SILENCING JOB

Walking Through the Valley

KOURTNEY GOVRO

WESTBOW
PRESS®
A DIVISION OF THOMAS NELSON
& ZONDERVAN

This book is a work of non-fiction. Unless otherwise noted, the author and the publisher make no explicit guarantees as to the accuracy of the information contained in this book and in some cases, names of people and places have been altered to protect their privacy.

WestBow Press books may be ordered through booksellers or by contacting:

WestBow Press
A Division of Thomas Nelson & Zondervan
1663 Liberty Drive
Bloomington, IN 47403
www.westbowpress.com
844-714-3454

Because of the dynamic nature of the Internet, any web addresses or links contained in this book may have changed since publication and may no longer be valid. The views expressed in this work are solely those of the author and do not necessarily reflect the views of the publisher, and the publisher hereby disclaims any responsibility for them.

Any people depicted in stock imagery provided by Getty Images are models, and such images are being used for illustrative purposes only. Certain stock imagery © Getty Images.

Scripture quotations are taken from the Holman Christian Standard Bible®, Used by Permission HCSB ©1999,2000,2002,2003,2009 Holman Bible Publishers. Holman Christian Standard Bible®, Holman CSB®, and HCSB® are federally registered trademarks of Holman Bible Publishers.

ISBN: 978-1-6642-6348-2 (sc)
ISBN: 978-1-6642-6349-9 (hc)
ISBN: 978-1-6642-6347-5 (e)

Library of Congress Control Number: 2022906823

Print information available on the last page.

WestBow Press rev. date: 5/7/2022

CONTENTS

DEDICATION

To my sweet wonderful husband, David. Thank you for walking through the valleys with me. Thank you for loving my family through tragedy and pulling us all back together. Thank you for being a man after God's own heart and demonstrating to our boys what it means to be the spiritual head of our house.

DEDICATION

INTRODUCTION

"You are just a Job," my mom said to me one day when I told her my latest folly and trial while we were sitting in a restaurant. In a lot of ways, she was right. Bad things seemed to seek me out, over and over. I lived in the valley, and if it could rain, it did, which would cause a flood. However, as I got older and read the book of Job, I could hardly compare myself to him. Most of my trials were self-inflicted.

Like many of you reading this, my life seemed to be a nonstop roller coaster of difficult seasons. While my friends appeared to have long luxurious summers, my life seemed different. I would barely get to spring before a surprise snow would fall and freeze whatever had started to grow. Maybe that is you too?

I secretly wished my Biblical spirit animal was someone other than Job—maybe someone like Esther, who was beautiful and just had to be bold. I could totally own that! Give me beauty, then let me do my bold thing. Alas, that was not my path. I was Job. In my mind, he was a short, heavy-set, middle-aged balding guy who wore white tube socks with his sandals and cried a lot. Sadly, that sounds similar to me.

A counselor once told me that I was creating my own brutal winters, and I needed to "silence Job."

But what did that mean?

She meant that "stinkin' thinkin'" was creating my sorrows, and I was manifesting all the bad in my life. The more I thought about being Job, the more I created Job-esque situations. While I believe that attitude is important, I do not believe you can manifest certain situations. You cannot create cancer or give your husband a heart attack just by thinking negative thoughts.

The dichotomy of an all-powerful, all-loving God versus the concept of suffering is hard to swallow. If He is a heavenly parent, and loves us so much, then why all of this? Why the bad? Why the pain? Why? During a conversation with one of my friends, who happens to be an atheist, he said "I couldn't believe in a God who…" It hit me. It would be easier not to believe in God than to understand His unlimited power and sovereignty. If He created the world, then why does He let bad things happen? If He is all-powerful, then why doesn't he stop the gauntlet of trying times? If He is all-knowing, then why doesn't He see bad things coming and redirect us? If He really is the great healer, then why do people we love get sick and die?

After a particularly difficult season, I took a risk and told a friend that I was questioning God in my suffering. She herself was going through an intense trial. In my mind, if anyone would wallow in suffering with me, it would be her. Maybe we would not just wallow, maybe she would even open a bottle with me so I could wash down my feelings from my head to my gut. Without hesitation or fumbling, she told me not to lose faith. God is bigger than anything she or I was experiencing. She rattled off scripture, framing God as the Creator, Sustainer, and Everlasting Hope. Then she said something like this: "If I believed God was just a person or a thing or an event, then I would've quit believing long ago. God is God, and I am not."

She did not try to explain my suffering; she redirected my focus. As you will see in the book of Job, sometimes that is all we need to do. These are a collection of devotions that I wrote at five a.m. each morning until I made it through the entire book of Job.

DAY 1

*Job...was a man of perfect integrity, who
feared God and turned from evil.*

—Job 1:2

When you study a book of the Bible, you need to approach it as a reporter would. Ask the W questions.

1. **When?** Scholars believe Job was the first book written in the Bible. It is physically located in the middle, right before Psalms, which is deceptive about its origin date. Actually, it is in a good spot—you need some psalms after this book. It is after the flood and before Jesus. (That's a little Bible humor for you—I thought it was witty.) It is set during the patriarchal period, which means that Job lived in the time around Abraham, Isaac, and Jacob.

2. **Where?** He lived in Uz (not to be confused with Oz). Today that is southern Israel.

3. **Who?** Now that is the meat of the story. Job was a real person, but his story reads like a fable. It is revered as one of the great literary pieces of all time. Even people who do not believe in God see the poetic structure of the book as incredible.

4. **Why?** The book of Job is in the Bible for a few reasons, but I believe its core purpose is to gain insight into God's sovereignty. *Sovereignty* is the most beautiful and awful word in the Bible. Sovereignty is God's authority and power over

everything. It is His providence and wisdom, which often do not appear to make sense. It is a complex concept—when "bad" things happen to "good" people. A book like Job needs a guide.

As a fellow valley walker, I will take you through what I have learned. Let's go through it together. Pray today that God will allow you to comfort someone. Read Job 1:1–5; tomorrow we will talk about Job the man.

DAY 2

As for me and my house we will worship Yahweh.

—Joshua 24:15b

JOB WAS A REGULAR GUY. THERE ARE DOZENS OF MEN TODAY LIKE HIM. This is one of the most important things to learn about Job, or the story becomes less fascinating. Job was a particularly good man, but the scripture says that he was a just man. He wasn't perfect nor was he someone without fault. He was just good.

Job was a dad. He took his role as the spiritual head of the household seriously. His kids were not always well behaved. It appears that they partied. In Job 1:4, his sons invited their sisters over to drink. Job got up early the next day and took them all home. Then he prayed over them. He demonstrated how to live a life honoring the Lord.

If I were to ask your kids, how do you know Mom or Dad loves the Lord, what would they say?

As a parent, I am responsible to teach my kids now more than ever. They are watching, us and learn more from our lives than. For example, I curse on occasion. It is a nasty habit. I am not a hardcore curser, but that is like saying I only sniff a little cocaine. One day, I heard one of my sons say some choice words. I had to take accountability for my part in that issue then wash his mouth out with soap.

The things we do are justified in our children's minds as acceptable, especially if we attend church and are generally good people. Job was mindful of that fact. He lived in a way that honored

God, both publicly and privately. When his children sinned, he took them through the process of repentance so they could learn. This was not because he was crazy or overbearing, but because he wanted to demonstrate how to live. His name is Job, and he is showing us our job.

Parenting is hard; parenting during a life crisis is harder. Someone needs to hear this. You are not alone in figuring it all out. God is here for you whenever you need Him, and even when you think you don't. Keep in the Word daily. Fill your tank. Pray today that God will help you be like Job, the parent. He will help you demonstrate to your kids a life that is honoring to God. What is God saying to you today?

DAY 3

The Lord asked Satan, "From where have you come from?" [Satan replied,] "From roaming through the earth and walking around on it."

—Job 1:7

WE STARTED WITH THE MAIN CHARACTER, JOB. I COULD PROBABLY GO on and on about him, but instead I will move on to the supporting actors. Let's start with the bad guy. You know every story needs a bad guy— the badder the better. I enjoy it when the author humanizes a bad guy, giving a backstory so that the character's badness is believable. The bad guy may even be on the edge of good. We all have a little bad guy in us. You do not teach a child to disobey; you teach him or her to obey. For a person to become a bad guy, the person is either nurtured or neglected in that direction.

When I started looking into Satan's backstory, I realized that what I knew about him was mostly just oral history. Oral history is what is said about someone or something, but there is no documentation to support it. For example, Satan is not a red man with horns; that is not in the Bible. He was once an angel. Wait, let me blow your mind here: humans do not become angels when they die. That is a myth. (Maybe you knew that. I didn't until a few years ago, and it was like *boom*!) Angels and humans are both created beings. They have different purposes. There are types and levels of angels—archangels, cherubim, and seraphim (maybe more). Scholars say that Ezekiel 28:14–19 is about him. It states that Satan was beautiful and powerful.

He wanted more. He wanted to be like God. It's like a twenty year-old kid who interviews for a job, and when asked what his five-year goal is, he replies, "To have your job." Satan wanted to be more powerful than God. Before you say, "Wow, he is awful," think of it this way…... When you choose your way over God's, you are saying the same thing. When you decide that your sin is okay because it is not that bad, you are saying the same thing that Satan said. Things that are "not that bad", like speeding, overeating, or cussing (ouch!) are all sins. Pray today that God would forgive you for the times you think your way is better than His way.

DAY 4

Let not the wise man boast in his wisdom; Let not
the strong man boast in his strength; Let not the
rich man boast in his riches. But him who boasts,
boasts in this—that he knows me, that I am Yahweh,
showing faithful love, justice, and righteousness
on the earth, for I delight in these things.

—Jeremiah 9:23–24

PRIDE IS THE ROOT OF ALL SIN. PRIDE IS THINKING YOU ARE BETTER than others. Worse, pride is assuming you are better than God. Pride was and is Satan's biggest problem. Pride is why he was cast out of heaven. It is the ultimate case of the grass being greener on the other side. He wanted the spotlight on him and convinced others to follow. Can't you hear him? "Who does God think he is?" While we may not say it out loud, we express it. We express it when something does not go the way we think it should or when a door closes that we think should be open. We express it when a prayer supposedly goes unanswered. It is undoubtedly one of the sins that God has had to work on with me.

The opposite of pride is humility. Humility is not self-depreciation. Humility is not talking poorly about yourself. Being humble is thinking of yourself less often than you think about others. It is putting yourself in a position to realize that your wisdom, strength, and riches are gifts. My husband was writing out a tithe check the other day, and he said, "It's easy to do because it's not ours anyway. Everything we have is a gift, and we are just shepherds of that gift." The prideful mindset says, "We worked hard for that money; our experience and knowledge and education put us in a position to earn it." Yes, I did my part, but God is the one who really did it all. He gave us the gift of brains, positioned us where we would be successful, and opened (or closed) doors to direct our paths. Those are statements of humility.

It took me many years, and some war wounds, to learn those things. I still struggle with pride. Pray today that God will open your eyes to pride in your life and that He will reveal how to let go of that attachment. When an opportunity presents itself to boast, turn it back to God. Boast of His blessing, His wisdom, and His strength.

DAY 5

Satan answered the Lord, "Does Job fear God
for nothing? Haven't you placed a hedge around
him, his household, and everything he owns?"

—Job 1:9–10a

MAKE SURE TO READ JOB 1:6–12. MY YOUNGEST IS A CHORE GUY. HE likes to have a list and to be paid. He is not opposed to bathrooms or dusting. He struggles with the list of things he must do—washing his own laundry, cleaning his room, picking up dishes, and taking out the trash—regardless of pay. He likes options. This way he can pick what he wants to do. We all have a little of that in us; a little bit of control goes a long way.

Like all the angels, Satan had a job to do. He had a role and tasks that were assigned by God. He did not want the job that he was assigned—he wanted to be the assigner. When that did not work, he appointed himself the adversary *and* the accuser. That is another form of pride. When we assign ourselves tasks of life, when God has laid out the way we should go, that is pride. Maybe we think the tasks are easier, or maybe they are less public and not Instagram picture material. Maybe they are tasks that put us at risk for public humiliation, such as sharing the gospel with someone. Regardless, when we turn down a role to which God is clearly calling us, we are doing exactly what Satan did. Satan decided his job was to create strife and trouble for the ones God loves the most.

What hurts you more as a parent: when you are hurting or when

9

your children are hurting? If Satan could not beat God, he was going to go after the thing that God loves the most: us. Read Job 1:10–11 again. Satan's end goal was to create enough separation between Job and God that God would lose a beloved child. But God knew Job's heart, and He knew that regardless of the situation, Job would not turn away. Would God say that about you? Or is your relationship with Him fragile? Pray today that God will reveal areas where you are fragile. If you are in the middle of the storm, will you allow me to pray for you?

DAY 6

Do you not know? [!] Have you not heard? [!]
Yahweh [God] is the everlasting God; [!] the Creator
of the whole earth; [!] He never grows faint or
weary; [!] there is no limit to His understanding [!]

—Isaiah 40:28

OH, I AM SO EXCITED! I COULD HARDLY WAIT TO GET OUT OF BED THIS morning. Today, we get to talk about my favorite character in the book of Job: God. I have more notes on Satan, but I am done with him. I need me some God. I want you to go back and read that verse again, with the exclamation points that I added. Okay, do it again, out loud! I get goose bumps each time. The word *everlasting* is the Hebrew word *olam*, which means forever, always, continuously existent, and perpetual. I will add never-ending and without beginning. God was there before time, is through all of time, and will be there after time ceases. He is everlasting. Does that overwhelm you? The God we worship is always, forever, and without end.

Take some time and meditate on the word *everlasting*. There is nothing hokey about meditation. It simply means to sit quietly, breathe deeply, clear your mind of distractions, and focus. Christian meditation does not clear your mind to nothing. We clear our mind of distractions like task lists, the barking dog, worries, and stresses. Then we focus on an attribute of God. He is everlasting. There was never a moment in time when He was not there. There was never a moment in your life when He was not available to you.

I know some of you are in the valley. Some of you are hurting so badly that you cannot imagine God anywhere in your vicinity. He is there and available. Some of you have been thrown into a valley, but are not able to walk through it. You collapsed in it, then could not find your way out. So you set up camp and took residence. He is everlasting, and He is there with you. Even as the rains come and floods overtake you, and the drought dries and parches you to cracking, He is there holding you, crying with you, and loving you. He is there with you when you are on top of the mountain, when everything is in perfect sequence and alignment. He is there celebrating with you. He is everlasting! Nothing can stop Him! Nothing can defeat Him! Nothing can erase His impact!

DAY 7

"Do you not know? Have you not heard?
Yahweh is the everlasting God; Creator of the
whole earth; He never grows faint or weary;
there is no limit to His understanding."

—Isaiah 40:28

I AM AN AVID HIGH SCHOOL BASKETBALL FAN. THE PROBLEM IS I HAVE four boys, and none of them likes basketball. Now, the tall one plays, but as he reminds me often, he does it for me. I have gotten better over the years, but referee heckling is a sport unto itself. Yes, yes, in all my Christian love, I sometimes cannot stop myself from helping the refs. I will admit we are so glad to play right now that rarely do I offer my services to the refs. Refs have an interesting job, not to mention awful outfits. They must know the rule book very well *and* be able to apply it in action. Wisdom, by human definition, is the act of blending experience and knowledge in action. That is what refs do, and no matter of heckling will change a call once it has been made. For the four quarters of the game, he or she is in charge. As soon as a penalty is called, it's called.

God's wisdom is different. His wisdom is a trait, not an acquired skill. In this scripture, when it says there is no limit to His understanding, that means application of both wisdom and knowledge. His knowledge is different than ours. He wrote the rulebook, and He knows how the game will go before it starts. He

13

allows every obstacle we face so that we can be refined into who we are meant to become.

Our boys have lost almost every week, but they still take the court. With six players on the team, it can be a long, grueling game. They are learning humility this year, over and over. My son says it will make winning that much sweeter when it comes. God, in His infinite wisdom and limitless understanding, put this experience in their lives *so that* at some point they will know how to honorably suffer defeat and rejoice in every victory. There is no limit to God's understanding. He knows the why of your circumstances. I know it is hard when you feel like you are losing every single time. I have been there, too. God is going to get you through it. God is never going to leave you. This circumstance will mold you into a better person if you allow it—if you choose it.

DAY 8

"In the beginning God created the
heavens and the earth."

—Genesis 1:1

THE FINAL WORD FROM THE VERSE IN ISAIAH 40:28 IS CREATOR. Creation is one of the reasons I believe. When I share the gospel with others, often I start with creation. If the world can unwind God as Creator in the minds of men, then it is hard to believe anything else. People who make quilts come in two general categories – those who love a pattern and those who wing it. When I started quilting, I enjoyed looking at a quilt then trying to figure out how to make it without a pattern. Or sometimes I would take an old quilt and try to fix it by removing a seam and replacing a piece.

Have you ever looked at the world that way and tried to figure out how it was made? Have you ever tried to trace the worlds seams and figure out how it all went together?

Scientists have done this, and do this today. Honestly, the only way they can really describe everything here is as a cosmic accident. This earth is not replicated in any way on any other planet within our reach. It is unique in every single aspect. If I stare at even a piece of creation long enough, I cannot figure out how He made it. Some of you might say that genetics, atoms, molecules are a complex puzzle. But that's the thing: the words *create* and *creator* originate from the Hebrew word *bara*. It means created by God. It is only used when referring to something He created. We cannot create the things God

15

created. We can study them and learn their attributes. Some things we can replicate but we cannot create from nothing. They are not like quilt blocks. Thank God for *bara* all things. Spend some time and list anything you can think of that He created, such as air, dirt, trees, and animals (even Taco, my dog). Spend some time meditating on God being *Bara*.

DAY 9

"Then God said..."

—Genesis 1:3a, 1:9a, 1:14a, 1:20a, 1:24a, and 1:26a

IT MIGHT TAKE YOU SOME TIME, BUT READ ALL OF GENESIS 1 TODAY. If you do not have a Bible, download the free YouVersion Bible app. Like most of us, I daily check email and my digital calendar for what I am to do that day. Over the past twenty years, that has included looking for what meetings I need to attend and what tasks I need to get done; and then there are the daily logistics of determining, with my husband, who will get which kid to which practice, game, or event. My weekends were spent packing for the next time I was to board a plane, check into a hotel, and figure out if I was flying to the right city. The best part of my travel weeks was looking for the funny things to post in my Skinny Knees mini blog to make others laugh. Generally, my calendar has been packed and I have been a slave to the fifteen-minute warning it provides. Are you like that? Maybe you don't have flights and meetings. I am home more now, and I wonder how we ever managed all of it.

As I have entered a new chapter of my life, this phrase struck me. Every single day of creation started out with, "Then God said." Read it with emphasis and excitement on *then*. Imagine the storyteller is so excited that he cannot wait to tell you what happened next. Sister, that is what God is doing every single day of your life! You get up and your day starts with "Then God said," and He has planned your entire day, week, month, year, life! We need to look for it, listen to it, and align with His vision. How do you do that? You open the Word of God so that He can speak to you. You pray. Allow your mind to be filled with Him. Listen to Christian radio. Talk to other believers.

After that, is the word *let*. This is super important to understand before reading the book of Job. Nothing happens without His knowledge. I know that is hard to take in sometimes. As you get up today and check your calendar, think about the phrase "Then God said." What is He saying to you this day, this month, this year? You got this, Sister, because God's got this!

DAY 10

"And God saw it was good."

—Genesis 1:12, 18, 21, 25, and 31

GOOD IS AN INTERESTING WORD. IN OUR BRAINS, WE PAIR IT WITH ITS opposite: *bad*. If something is not good, then the opposite would be bad. The word *ken* is Hebrew for good, but it also means to be loved. That makes sense, right? God made things, sat back, looked at them and said, "I did a good job." This verse isn't God patting Himself on the back for a job well done. It is an expression of love. We put our human eyes on that experience. We imagine the world as He created it, in utter perfection. He defines that beautiful world and people as good. But the reality is that people are born selfish. If not, Eve would have never bitten the fruit. How is that good? How is someone who would disobey the God who gave her everything and more - good? We are not good. By our very nature, we are all different degrees of bad, all with a tendency, like Satan, to think that our way could be better. Good does not mean right. Good means loved.

I spent my younger years trying to be the good girl, believing that my goodness was tied somehow to my worth. It is not. Your worth— your value—is tied to God. He sits back and looks at you every single day and says, "She is good. She is my creation. She was built for great things. I made her with intention and purpose." I am loved from day one to the day I get to go home to be with Him. Quit tying your worth to what you are doing and start affixing your worth to Who created you. Surrender the need to be "good enough" because you never will get there. God provided a path to wholeness through His Son, Jesus. The path to wholeness starts with admitting that you are not whole and cannot get there on your own. Then you ask God to forgive your decisions to put yourself before Him; this is called sin. The final step is just to believe and commit to knowing him better every day. Quit beating yourself up. You are good. You are loved.

DAY 11

"And it was so..."

—Genesis 1:7, 9, 11, and 24

THIS, FOR ME, IS BOTH THE MOST WONDERFUL AND DIFFICULT PHRASE in the entire Bible. This is God's power to do or not to do summed up in four little words. They are not even fancy words. They are casual words by all accounts. However, when put in this sequence and in the context of this chapter, they are powerful. Genesis 1 eases us into the concept of sovereignty. Sovereignty is defined by *Merriam-Webster* as "supreme power or authority." It is easy to accept the idea of that through the creation of the world. God spoke, it happened, and He said, "That's good." Creation is beautiful and magical and satisfying.

It is the song "So Will I" in loud worship: "If the rocks cry out your greatness, so will I!" I can stare at the oceans, mountains, or anything, and see the beauty of God's work and know He is powerful. He made all of this out of nothing and therefore He controls it. Who decided to tell the ocean you can only go this far onto the shore? Who pulled the mountains up from the plains? Who let the lava flow from a volcano to create the tropical island paradise? God did—but think that through. Who commands the sky to open and let the rain fall so much that it floods, or withholds it from our farms? Who allows the wind to whip into a funnel and destroy a town, or blow so hard it picks up the ocean and hurls it onto the shore? Who steps back when the sea sends a wave that sucks inhabitants from the land into the watery depths?

"And it was so" is a difficult phrase to consume. It is a difficult phrase to accept when you are not in Sunday school looking at a felt board with happy birds and trees. It is a phrase that means no matter what, He is in control. As we study Job, you will start to unwrap this idea that nothing happens without His knowing or allowing it. That is both a wonderful and difficult concept. The God who created the universe is on your side, but He intends to help you grow. Pray today that God will open your heart to the phrase "And it was so." Pray today that in your waiting, in your suffering, in your joy, and in your wins, you will see God's hand.

DAY 12

"Have you considered my servant Job?"

—Job 1:8

I HAVE BEEN CONSIDERING THE PURCHASE OF A LONG ARM QUILTING machine. For the non-quilting readers, that is the sewing machine that puts the front and back of the quilt together and stitches the patterns across the quilt. Most quilters do what is called piecing: sewing the different fabrics together. Very few do long-arming. It is kind of an art. Once you finish your quilt you send it off to be quilted by someone with a coveted machine. Quilting costs about one and a half cents per square inch or more, so a queen-size quilt can cost more than $100. Good long-arming is totally worth it. As I consider what to do, I determine how many quilts I make each month. Can I do the quilting step myself? Do I want to? Is that a piece of the art of quilting I want to do? The last question, which is the biggest, is do I want to make that investment in the actual long arm machine? It costs more than my first car.

To consider something means to carefully think about it before deciding. We are going to work through this scripture for a few days because it is probably the most difficult one in the entire book of Job. It is repeated in Job 2. I will admit, I skipped over it for years, but when I committed to studying the book of Job last year the verse shocked me. In this verse, God talks to Satan. "Have you considered" (thought about or examined before making a decision) "my servant

Job." Satan was looking for ways to cause trouble—that is who he is at his core. God suggested Job. Satan did not bring up Job—God did.

Before you see the trials in this chapter, this verse is everything. It changes the entire perspective on Job's suffering, and it should change yours. God, in His wisdom and sovereignty, asks Satan if he has considered Job.

The opposite of the word *consider* is to dismiss or look away. What is something you have considered lately? A purchase? A job change? A relationship? Think about your process. What does it mean to consider something? Take some time today to write your thoughts about this word *considered*. Pray that God will open your heart to understanding.

DAY 13

"Have you considered my servant Job?"

—Job 1:8

MY YOUNGEST USED TO CALL SERVING ONE ANOTHER "BUTLERING." He would use it as a verb, such as, "I don't want to butler that," or at times he would say, "I am not your butler." I would often explain that in this family, we butler for one another, especially when Mom says so. To be great in this household, he needed to be the butler of all.

The word *servant* has a similar definition to his concept of "butler." The word in Hebrew is *ebed*, which means a fully committed, helpful follower. In Mark 9:35, Jesus tells the Twelve that to be great in God's kingdom, you must be a servant of all. The Greek word for servant is *diakonos*, which means one who executes the commands of another. The word hearkens to the idea of humbleness and sacrifice or willingness to do whatever God has called you to do. Reword this scripture with these definitions: "Have you considered [thought about, examined] my servant [humble, committed, follower, who does what I tell him to do] Job?" God is not referring to someone who is half-committed or just meandering along, occasionally dropping in on church, or when he or she has time, listening to a YouTube sermon. No, He is referring to someone who is all in and holding nothing back. This person is devoted: giving his or her tithe, volunteering in ministry, praying daily, the Word of God oozing from the person's mouth at any moment, singing with Christian radio in the car, fully 100 percent committed. Do you get it? God is asking

Satan to consider making trouble in the life of someone we should all aspire to be!

Christianity is not a free pass for easy. There is nothing easy about this world. In this life you will have pain, loss, illness, hurt, and suffering. We are going to see that Job suffered beyond what anyone could ever earn. So not only does this scripture have to establish that he did nothing wrong, he lived right, and God put it out there to the enemy to consider him. It is heavy stuff, but I promise that God does not leave. He is ever present in times of suffering. Pray today and ask God, "Am I your servant?" Ask God, "Would you consider me *ebed* or *diakonos?*"

DAY 14

*"For I am God, and there is no other; I am God, and
no one is like Me. I declare the end from the beginning,
and from long ago to what is not yet done, saying
My plan will take place, and I will do all My Will."*

—Isaiah 45:9b–10

DISCUSSING GOD'S SOVEREIGNTY IS IN SOME WAYS EASY, AND IN SOME ways one of the most difficult topics. *Sovereignty* means supreme power and authority. Nothing happens that is unknown, and nothing happens that is unplanned. As humans, we justify suffering and rationalize it. *If* You are so powerful and *if* You love me so much, why are You letting me hurt? Job spends most of the book in this state. In some ways, we want to categorize suffering in our minds, and determine whether it is earned or unearned. We justify suffering based on life events, and say it is punishment or refinement. If I suffer, then I learn something. Both of those are valid, and Job would learn more humility. But did he need to suffer to learn? Job 1:8 states that God said of Job, "he has perfect integrity and feared God." It is hard to get better than perfect integrity, right? Job's suffering was unearned. Shouldn't suffering be an if/then? If I do something or if I need to learn something, then I will suffer? Doesn't that make more sense? Why did Job suffer? What in his life needed refinement, or what had he done to earn it? Nothing!

Sovereignty is not fortune telling. It is not seeing into the future. The verse today says, "I declare the end from the beginning, and from long ago to what is not yet done. My plan will take place, and I will do all my Will." Sovereignty is more than knowing; it is owning and planning. I am going to spoil the ending for you: Job never did learn why he suffered, at least not while he was on earth. God never gave the reason to him. Part of faith is being okay with not knowing, and I would contend, not understanding the ways of God. It is being okay with someone else saying of your life, "My (not your) plan will take place." Your suffering may not be about you. Sister, that is hard, and that is what He is teaching you today. Pray today that God will comfort you through that learning.

DAY 15

"Very well," the Lord said to Satan, "everything
he owns is in your power. However, you
must not lay a hand on Job himself."

—Job 1:12

GETTING LOST IS A REGULAR EVENT WHEN I AM DRIVING. SOMETIMES I do not use the GPS because I think I know where I am going. Sometimes I use the GPS but disagree with the route. On occasion, I get so lost that I call my husband. He will ask, "Do you have your GPS set?" My reply is usually, "If I had set it, would I be calling you?" (Our life is often like a sitcom.) If you turn on the GPS, it will get you to the destination. It may not take the route you think you should go. Sometimes it reroutes because of road work, but ultimately it will get you there. Sometimes I feel like God has placed a GPS on my life, and I keep rerouting myself. I am going to end up where He wants me to end up, but it may take me longer to get there than it could have, had I just listened.

Sometimes the GPS will take you through places where the road is messed up with potholes or even hazards. That is how I see this verse. God, in His supreme authority (sovereignty), gives Satan permission to engage. In some ways that is awful, right? God is giving Satan permission to do incredibly awful things to Job. In other ways, that is amazing. God has control over Satan, as well as over our God-given routes. Remember the verse from yesterday: "My plan will take place" (Isaiah 46:10). Satan can do nothing without

God's permission. That is heavy, but balance that out with other scripture. He loved us enough to die for us (Romans 5:8). In the Old Testament, He parted the Red Sea, told Noah to build a boat, dropped a giant with a slingshot, closed the mouths of lions, let men dance in the fire, brought down walls by the blowing of horns, and so much more. He is in full control and faithful to deliver us here on earth, or if you have Jesus as your best friend, when you get to heaven. You win no matter what happens. I know suffering is hard; I have had my share in the last few years as I watched people I love suffer. Quit trying to set your course and just listen to the GPS. Pray that God will open your heart to His course for your life.

DAY 16

*"Satan answered the Lord, "Does
Job fear God for nothing?""*

—Job 1:9

I DO NOT LIKE SCARY MOVIES, HAUNTED HOUSES, OR ANYTHING OF that genre. I do not pay to be scared. I can turn the news on and get the same effect for free. I am the Ebenezer Scrooge of Halloween. Bah Humbug! I do not appreciate scary. In the English language, we lump the word *fear* into the category of scared or afraid. *Merriam-Webster* even defines it is an emotion linked to danger and giving its synonyms as creeps, jitters, and apprehension. It is no wonder that when you read "fear the Lord," it is confusing. Fear is identified as an emotion and not a state of being. The antonyms (opposites) for it are the words brave or courageous. In our culture those are honorable and noble words that can be used to describe someone. Who does not want to be viewed as being brave? That is where our language and the original have some translation limitations.

The word *fear* in Hebrew is *yare*, which means to respect, reverence, or be aware of awesome power. Think of it linked to the word *humble*: I am not afraid; I just recognize He is God, and I am not. I do not fear God like one might fear Freddy or Jason or some other scary movie character. I fear God because He is God and He created everything on this earth. He decides the rise and fall of kings. He flooded the world when the world became too awful. He sent fire from heaven to silence the prophets of Baal. He split the sea so the Israelites could escape the Egyptians. He is more powerful than anything in this universe or any other. He is sovereign and controls yesterday, today, and tomorrow. I am not afraid of Him. I do not cower and hide from Him because I balance the power He has with the knowledge that He sent His Son to die for me. He wants to have a relationship and He loves me. That is what fear is. It is not being afraid. It is the balance of knowing He is in control of it all *and* He loves me more than any human could ever love me. Meditate on God's awesome power and God's awesome love today.

DAY 17

"But stretch out your hand and strike everything he owns, and he will surely curse you to your face."

—Job 1:11

I HAVE FOUR BOYS. WHEN THEY WERE LITTLE AND GOT IN TROUBLE (which was often), one of the most effective punishments was to take away a toy (or all of the toys). I would pack them up and put them in my bedroom. That still works today, but now it is phones, computers, and cars. One day, the youngest did something, and I took his entire set of superhero action figures. He was devastated and fell on the ground throwing a fit. (I added time to the timer for that stunt.) In his tears and sorrow, he explained these were his best friends, and he needed them. He gave several reasons why this was too harsh. I will admit that there have been several times in the last few years when God took something or someone away from me and I threw a fit. When I lost things, it was hard and I was bitter.

However, when it came to losing people, that is when pain pushed me over the edge. In my pain, I struggled to open my Bible, and at the hardest times even struggled to go to church. It was hard to see others in joy when I was in sorrow.

Satan looks for things that we are attached to. He knows that through attachment he can create more pain. Attachment is the idea that if I lose something, then I will be in pain. Attachment is dangerous, but it is human. A lot of New Age religions teach that if you are attached to nothing then you can never hurt because attachment is the core of pain. In some ways that is true, and you can even make some Biblical arguments for it. The Bible teaches that you should love God most, above and beyond anything else (Matthew 27:3). It teaches that losing things and people *is* very painful, but in that pain, we have a Comforter. It teaches us to love our neighbors as ourselves. It teaches not to put the love of people or things in front of your love for God. Satan believed that if he took things that Job was attached to, then Job would turn his back on God. The attachment would win. It is a hard question, but is that true of you? Are there things or people in your life that, if you lost them, would cause you to curse God to his face? Pray today that God will reveal that to you.

DAY 18

"I alone have escaped to tell you."

—Job 1:15b, 16b, 17b, and 19b

SEVERAL YEARS AGO, I HEARD A WOMAN NAMED CHRISTINE SPEAK about her experience as a victim of sex trafficking. I am reminded of this in this passage in Job. She shared one horrific story after another of abuse, illness, deaths of friends, humiliation, and judgement. Her book, *Cry Purple*, is one everyone should read. As I was reading Job 1:13–19, she came to mind. Sometimes we escape things so that we can report. The word *tell* in Hebrew is *nagad*, which means to make known or to announce. It is more than telling; it is reporting. In my mind, I see breathless servants running to Job. The servants were probably physically bruised from their experiences. The scripture states that the servants escaped. They did not just watch; they were part of that tragedy. Job heard it all, but the servants saw it all. The word *escaped* in Hebrew means something like a spark leaping from a flame. As we live through tragedy, we are like sparks leaping from a flame. A spark, if it hits a fertile surface, will ignite another flame. That is what Christine has done. She leaped from her tragedy, shared her story, and ignited the flame to help others.

That is what God wants us to do with our tragedies. Fire can consume us, or it can make us like the spark that leaps to escape and starts a new flame. Christine is like the flame that ignites real change. Pray today for some warriors in the fight against sex trafficking. Pray for Restoration House and others working to help those who are experiencing that pain. their work. Pray that God will encourage your heart to be a spark. If you are going through, or have been through tragedy, do not sit and smolder. Be a spark that escapes to share and help others.

DAY 19

"Naked I came from my mother's womb, and
naked I will leave this life. The Lord gives and the
Lord takes away. Praise the Name of Yahweh."

—Job 1:21

THIS IS ANOTHER TOUGH VERSE TO GET THROUGH IN JOB. JOB 1:12 IS a statement of sovereignty. Job 1:21 is seen as Job's reaction to sovereignty. In many ways, this is an example of how we should react or at least desire to react to God's sovereignty. Make sure to read verse 20. I think we skip that verse because verse 21 is so poetic and is often converted into popular songs. Verse 20 is Job's real reaction to the news: he tears his clothes, shaves his head, and falls to the ground.

Have you ever gotten bad news? The shock of it can feel like a literal punch in the gut. Later, it may hit you out of the blue, through a song or something else that invokes the memory and a similar response. Sometimes it is not as visceral, but it is still there. I tell you that because you need to know that you are normal. Loss hurts, and while you may not need to get over it, you do need to continue.

God chose to keep you here for a reason. God has a purpose for you. We are His creation, created in Christ Jesus for good works, which God prepared for us ahead of time. When life gives us more than we can humanly handle, we look to God. Maybe, once we get through our initial grief, we need to start asking, "Why did you leave me here? What is my purpose?" That event, that pain, should not define you. You are more than a moment, an event, and more than pain. Use pain as a fork in the road. You get to choose. Do I use this moment to launch me to great things? Do I use this moment as an excuse to sit in sorrow? Sister, I know it is hard. It is okay to be in pain, it is okay to cry, and it is okay to just be overwhelmed. Just do not choose to live there. God has a good plan for you, and He is there to help you accomplish it. Pray today that God will help you move to where He wants you to be. Find someone to share your struggle with, pray with, and be connected to.

DAY 20

"I am not saying this out of need, for I have learned
to be content in whatever circumstances. I know
both how to have a little and how to have a lot."

—Philippians 4:11–12a

MY YOUNGEST HAD SEVERAL CLEANING PROJECTS THIS WEEKEND SO he could earn $25 for ordering 500 cards for his game. He has the same tendencies that I do with hobbies. It is not enough to have a few or understand a little—we go all in. I have made nearly thirty quilts in eight months. I read books and patterns, talked to people, bought software so I could design my own quilts, and researched how fabric manufacturers worked. I come by it honestly—just ask my dad about maps.

A few years ago, I studied the word *enough*. The word means as much or as many as required. We do not get to define enough, because being content means being okay even when we do not think we have enough. It is another lesson in sovereignty, God's control over everything. He gives and He takes. He allows. Job said, "naked I came and naked I go." (We did not have anything when we arrived, and we don't take anything with us.) The Lord gives and He takes away. What we have is not ours anyway.

In Philippians 4, Paul gave God praise. He said, "I am content whether in little or in much." Do not get so focused on the learning around suffering in Job that you miss the learning around contentment. I will tell you after a year of study on the word *enough*,

I still struggle with it. It is my need for control more than a desire for more. However, as frustrated as I may get with circumstances, I have found I would rather do life with God than without. I would rather fall on my knees in praise and prayer than suffer in solitude. Pray today that enough will be God's enough for you. Pray today that you will find peace in whatever His enough for you today is.

DAY 21

*"Throughout all of this Job did not sin
or blame God for anything."*

—Job 1: 21

I STRUGGLE WITH THIS VERSE. JOB WENT THROUGH THREE MASSIVE trials and had every opportunity to "curse God to his face" or flip God off, as Satan predicted. Yet he didn't. Maybe it is a little jealousy. I mean I certainly have not handled all my trials with such grace and fortitude. Many times, I dealt with trials in unhealthy and destructive ways. I could only wish to be like the grumpy and frustrated Job of the middle of this book. That depression would have been more constructive than my old habits of dealing with pain.

The Hebrew word for sin in this scripture is *hata*, which means to miss the way to go or miss the mark. People often bristle at the word sin because they feel judged for their actions. Some say, "The Bible is just a rule book telling me all the ways I am bad." Let me challenge your thinking a bit. Sin, or the things described as sin, in the Bible are the lines on the highway or guard rails. When you are driving down the road, the goal is to stay between the lines. Why? Well, if you go off to the side then the road is bumpy and unfinished. You can still drive on it, but it is dangerous. You could drive over the center line, but you risk a head-on collision. You could try to drive across the median, but you risk an even larger accident. Many obstacles and boundaries are put there to protect. Trials and stress can cause us to want to cross the road lines, using unhealthy or destructive ways to deal with those things. We may even numb our feelings for a while.

Job did the opposite. He surrendered it. He praised God in his storm. He recognized God's power. He relinquished his pain to God. I get it—totally and completely. If you are reading this and thinking that's unrealistic, that is okay. It is okay to be human and sad and hurt. Sweet sister, it is not okay to be destructive to yourself. Cry out to God – He already knows you are upset. Pray today and let it all out. Whatever it is, whatever your burden is, let it all out to God.

DAY 22

"He still retains his integrity, even though you invited
me against him, to destroy him without just cause."

—Job 2:3b

WE LOST A LOT OF BASKETBALL GAMES THIS SEASON. IT HAS BEEN tough. Most of our team is young and inexperienced. Most teams in our league realized quickly and played their second string against our six- or seven-man team. But sometimes, they acted like Cobra Kai and showed little mercy. My number two son took on a leadership role, and in one game lost his cool, yelling at a ref and earning a technical foul. We had a long talk about it that night. A few games later, we played a very unevenly matched game. Their coach pressed every time, and the kids laughingly dunked on our kids. Mama was going to lose her cool on that coach after the game. The final score was 89 to 8. I watched my big guy walk over, fist bump the other team, thank them for coming, and tell them how impressed he was with their skill. The other team, shocked, shook his hand and returned the compliment. Some of the younger players followed him and imitated him, so did I.

Job went through incredible trials, and God said of him, "he retained his integrity." The word *retain* is *hazaq* in Hebrew, which means to fasten on. When I put on a belt, I choose to put it on. I choose to fasten it. It does not just magically appear. I choose whether to secure it tightly or just put it on loose. The same is true with integrity and character. We get to decide if integrity is our way or not. Integrity is doing the right thing when no one, except God, is looking. It is choosing to do the right thing, even when it is not easy. Constantly losing can make you bitter and angry, or you can choose to take the lessons and become better.

Last night, my son said to me, "This is a really good team we are playing. We don't have all of our players. I am going to make sure all the guys get a chance to score. That's my goal." One kid scored who hadn't scored this season; the crowd erupted with cheers. We lost, but we won. We get to decide our reaction to adversity, and we give glory and honor to God in our decision. Pray today that you will represent well, and honor God in adversity.

DAY 23

*"But stretch out your hand and strike his flesh and
bones, and he will surely curse You to Your face."*

—Job 2:5

IN JOB 2:4–8, WE SEE THE THIRD OF JOB'S TRIALS: PHYSICAL ILLNESS. His body is covered in oozing boils from his head to the bottom of his feet. I had early-stage cancer a few years ago, followed by a year of surgeries. It came on the heels of several other trials, like a divorce and some financial difficulties. This was a precursor to intense challenges with my husband's heart attack, some business challenges, family quarrels, the death of my brother—well, you get the picture. Satan believed he could break Job by attacking the only thing Job had left: his body. He had no money, he had no children, and as we are going to see in the next verse, even his wife left. What else did he have?

Job is not a story of learning dependency on God or even finding comfort from Him. During most of the book, God is silent to Job in his suffering. A theme in Job is identifying what is more important to us than God. It is about creating space to ask yourself the scary question: *if* this happens then what will I do? Satan is already asking that question, evaluating your weaknesses, and targeting them. Maybe it is blame or guilt that he will target in your suffering. Maybe it is pride. Maybe it is attachment. Look at that verse: "But" is followed by a recommendation for a trial. He is saying, "Wait, the last one did not work, but let's try this one."

Do you ever feel like that is what is happening to you? Satan is sitting there with a bag full of awful, and he keeps trying ways to break you? In those times, when doctors fail, the bank account is empty, or you are staring at a loved one in a hospital bed, fight back with prayer. Punch Satan right in the teeth with prayer. Girl, the God of the universe is on your side and His fist is flying for you. You may not see an immediate result, but Satan will feel it every single time. Pray today, and punch Satan in the mouth. It feels good to fight back.

DAY 24

"His wife said to him, "Do you still retain your integrity? Bless (Curse) God and die!"

—Job 2:9

PEOPLE GIVE MRS. JOB A REALLY HARD TIME, SAYING THAT SHE IS kicking Job when he is down. I think that is wrong. Do not forget that Mrs. Job just lost everything too: her home, her money, and worst of all, her children. And she was watching the man she loved suffer. Sometimes we put unrealistic expectations on people who are going through hard times. We expect them to say or do the "right" things. We expect them to show up pain free or at least be composed. Sisters, that is sin, and it is simply wrong. We should not judge someone's reaction to pain, because everyone is at a different point in his or her journey.

Maybe next time you are with someone who is clearly going through a trial, you could say, "I know you are hurting. I am going to pray for you, but what else can I do for you?" Do not have any expectations about the person's response. What does that mean? Do not get your feelings hurt if the person reacts poorly to your offer. That statement does three things. First, you acknowledge the other person's pain, and demonstrate that you understand. You may not know what it's like to lose someone, or have cancer, or lose a job, but you know it hurts. Sometimes people just need permission to feel hurt, not stuff it, and not just say, "I'm fine." The Bible does not advocate stoicism; it advocates grace.

Second, say what should be the obvious, "I am praying for you." If you aren't, then you start. You cannot fix the other person's hurt, but God can. Prayer has power to heal. The final thing is asking, "What can I do?" I am a Baptist and when bad things happen, our cultural response is to bring food. I used to make fun of that, but it is a beautiful tradition. Food is necessary and it brings comfort. The other person may need nothing, but your offer is important.

In 2020, I have seen friends lose children, friends lose husbands, and several lose parents. My family lost my brother. He was a father, husband, son, and dear friend. I have friends who are sick, have lost jobs, and are hurting. Mrs. Job (and, as we will find out later, Job's friends) teaches us that everyone will react differently. Be an example of God's grace. Pray today for someone who is hurting.

DAY 25

"They met together to go and sympathize
with him and comfort him."

—Job 2:11b

READ JOB 2:11–13. IN A PLAY, THE THREE FRIENDS WOULD ENTER stage right. They are kind of like Job's wife: they get a bad rap for being ill prepared and poor deliverers of comfort to their friend. God has a plan for everyone. Sometimes that plan is to allow us to look foolish, so that others can learn. Sometimes, it is so that we, ourselves, can learn how to be better. I think of how many times I privately took a learning from God. Can I just get an amen from all y'all out there who are glad we did not grow up with social media, where the world could see all our learning experiences? Amen, amen, and amen. Okay, back to the story.

Job's friends met together to sympathize, but as they approached, nothing prepared them for his sorrow. It was so overwhelming that they tore their robes and wept. Then they sat with him for seven days in silence, because they wanted to give him space and to allow him to speak first. Can you imagine that? A mourning friend, not a family member, stopping everything for seven full days to comfort with his presence. In the Jewish tradition, this is called *shiva*. The word *shiva* means seven and is still honored today. I used my phone-a-friend option on this and spoke to a few of my Jewish friends, including a Rabbi, to get some information. *Shiva* starts after burial and is held at the home of the deceased or a close family member. It is a beautiful tradition because it allows the family space to mourn as well as space to receive comfort. In our fast-paced culture, we often do not allow this for people who lose loved ones. The act of stopping and being still allows them time to process before the question, "How are you?" They are sad. You do not need to ask. Just say, "I am sorry," and be there. I think this is good practice for any major trauma. Why do we brush things aside when people are hurting? Why can't we just share space with those in pain? I get it: seven days is hard, seven hours is hard, but could you sit quietly with a hurting friend for seven minutes? I challenge you to be that person who shows up and is willing to take a day off work for a friend in pain.

DAY 26

"May the day I was born perish and the night
when they said, "A boy is conceived."

—Job 3:3

READ CHAPTER 3. WE ARE GETTING INTO A PART OF JOB THAT TAKES us down a rabbit hole of sadness. When I was younger, I heard someone tell someone who was mourning a loss to read Job. So I started saying it. Note that I had never read Job myself. I just heard a grown up say it, so I assumed it was a good idea. I have studied Job for the last few years and realized that wasn't great advice. If you are mourning, read the first three chapters and then skip to the end (chapters 38–42). Better yet, read some psalms and soak in some comfort. The book of Job is forty-two chapters long. Chapters 3 through 38, thirty-five chapters, are Job fussing, and his friends trying to figure out what he has done wrong to deserve the "punishment" he is receiving from God. Be careful. His friends are wrong. Job is hurting and spewing out pain.

I am so glad my journal is not on display for all to read. Girl, when I suffer, I write my prayers out to vomit my pain out of my body. It is a good practice. Sometimes I keep them and sometimes I throw them away. In Job's pain, he questions God's decision to bring him into the world. He wishes that he had never been born, because then he would never have had this pain. That is some real pain. You may disagree, but I think what he did is okay, God understands pain. He suffered more than anyone else when He carried the weight of the world's sin for all time and was brutally nailed to a cross. Jesus even asked God to change His mind. The difference is that Jesus humbly said, "Not my will, but yours."

Job's speeches are why I like Job; he is real. He fusses rather dramatically, and the author allows thirty-five chapters for it. Pain does not vanish overnight. The author does not downplay the reality of suffering. Most cannot say from day one, "God, this hurts, but I trust You," and wipe our tears and be good. You know what? That is okay. There was no one more wonderful than Job, according to God Himself in chapter 1. It took him thirty-five chapters to turn the corner. Pray today that you will give yourself grace in your suffering. Pray today, that if you are comforting a suffering friend, you will give that person space to hurt.

DAY 27

"In my experience, those who plow injustice
and those who sow trouble reap the same."

—Job 4:8

THERE IS A TEAM WE PLAY IN BASKETBALL. ONE OF THE PLAYERS HAS a ritual before he shoots a free throw that can only be described as a shimmy. Imagine a six foot three and more teenage boy walking up to the free throw line, dribbling, then wiggling his entire body before he shoots. It is one of the many delights I have when watching that team. The other is that they are well-coached, plus the players and parents are kind. The free throw ritual is part superstition, but also part muscle memory. As you go through the steps, theoretically your mind and body focus, then mechanically, you shoot the free throw, and make the basket. It is an if/then. Does it always work? No, but it does increase the probability of accuracy.

Eliphaz was the first of Job's friends to speak. Some scholars believe he was the oldest or most senior of the group. He employs a very logical train of thought, an if/then. It is like any scientific question or theory. If one thing happens, then it always causes another. If we see an effect, then clearly there must be a cause. It is like *karma*: the sum of someone's actions determines the future. Ah, but *karma* will not work with Job, because he has no cause or reason for suffering. Look at God's own Word. Reread Job 1:8 and Job 2:3. Eliphaz's logic is not absolute. The speeches of Job's friends, while wholly inappropriate to administer seven days after the loss of an entire family, are not unfounded in scripture. There are several examples of suffering because of sin. Galatians 6:7–9 is one of them; in it, Paul tells his audience that God is not mocked, and you reap what you sow.

But, just like shooting a free throw, you can do all the steps right and still miss. You can do all the healthy things and still have a heart attack or get cancer. You can be perfectly devout and still lose your job or a spouse. The point is we do not follow Christ because we think it is a free pass for a perfect life; it is not. Follow Christ because of what He did for you on the cross, and because He loved you so much He made a path to heaven. Follow Christ because the path He left includes loving the unlovable, and serving those who can never pay you back.

DAY 28

"A despairing man should receive loyalty from his friends, even if he abandons the fear of the Almighty."

—Job 6:14

THE WORD *LOYALTY* IS THE HEBREW WORD *HESED*, WHICH MEANS loving kindness. After two chapters of Eliphaz pontificating his stance that Job must have done something awful to deserve what he got, Job replies. After thirteen verses of Job saying that he still wishes he hadn't been born, he says in verse 14, "Can you be full of loving kindness and keep a friend accountable?" I think so.

Matthew 7:3–5 are verses that we have all used, but we usually stop at verse 3: "Judge not, lest ye be judged." (I prefer it in the King James when I am scolding someone for judgement—it comes across as more holy.) Sometimes we push further and use the next verses about not picking the speck out of someone's eye when we have a plank in our own. Oh, that one is good for putting someone who is trying to correct our behavior in his or her place. We just happen to leave out the end, the part that says once you remove the plank, you can see clearly to help your buddy with the speck.

Friends, Eliphaz was wrong for accusing Job in that moment of pain and sorrow, not to mention being so long winded in doing so. The Bible does teach us to keep one another accountable. I go to a chiropractor. She can feel around and figure out what is in and out of place, but she always starts by asking me how I am feeling. She has helped me learn to listen to my body. She has worked on me for several months. She is familiar with me, so she has a baseline. Before she adjusts me, she asks questions and references the baseline. Later that night she calls to check in. Isn't that a good model for accountability? You must invest in someone long enough to know the person's baseline and ask questions to understand his or her willingness for adjustment. Once you offer the truth in love, you gotta follow up! Don't drop the mic and exit stage left. That is not accountability; it is just being accusatory and hurtful. Friendship is not always lattes and laughs. It is helping one another love God more. Pray today that God will help you be a good friend. Find an accountability partner who fears God and will help you on your journey.

DAY 29

"For we walk by faith, not by sight, and
we are confident and satisfied to be out of
body and at home with the Lord."

—2 Corinthians 5:7

SOME MORNINGS I AM DISTRACTED BEYOND MY ABILITY TO GET through my Bible Study. Many days big dog and little dog decide it would be best if I focus on them and not the Bible. I was reminded of the days when my boys were littles. There are no peaceful moments in a house with four small boys. They do not sleep in when they are small. They do not stop for a few hours and play quietly. When they are quiet, bad things happen—things like putting their baby brother in a laundry basket and launching him down two flights of stairs. I read a Facebook post once from a mom who said something about "me time." Frazzled, I looked at my husband and said, "Me time? The only me time I get is pee time when I lock the door, and even then, they knock or stick their fingers underneath the door and beg to come in."

When number four was around one, I started getting up early to do a quiet time. Many mornings David would find me, my Bible, and a fat baby snoring in a chair, or me at the kitchen table drooling on my notepad. It took years before it became habit and even more years before it became like oxygen. Now, I cannot start my day without a moment with Jesus. When I was too tired to read, I listened to

Priscilla Shirer or Tim Keller. When I was too overwhelmed by the weight of the world, then I just sat, held my Bible, prayed, and cried.

The point of all this is we need to be kind to ourselves at different phases of life. God gets it. He gave you those kids (or dogs). God appreciates your efforts. Bible study is just about connecting with Him. There is no perfect way. That time can be five minutes or five hours. Don't be so hard on yourself. Pray today for personal grace and thank God for those babies or dogs, who sometimes distract you from your study. Pray for that young mom you know. I get it—it's tough. You can do it.

DAY 30

"Since your children sinned against Him,
He gave them over to their rebellion."

—Job 8:4

ALL OF JOB'S FRIENDS ARE STUCK ON THIS IDEA THAT JOB MUST HAVE sinned to deserve this. This is the idea of the law of if/then. Even Bildad said Job's kids got what they deserved. At that point, to quote my cousin Joi, I would have turned to the other friends and said, "Hold my hoops." I think Job showed amazing restraint. While the Bible does show God and His wrath, and consequences when sin occurs, we should not be focused on the consequence for a specific sin. We should focus on the consequences for all sin, which is the reason for separation from God Himself. The wages of sin is death. This does not mean earthly, bodily death. Everyone physically dies, regardless of sin. Romans 6:23 discusses ultimate separation from God Himself, from God's love, and His wholeness.

I had a conversation with an atheist friend yesterday. His daughter-in-law had received some extremely hurtful, and frankly unscriptural, condemnations from her religious family. It is so dangerous for the Christian community and Christians to judge others. It is hard to speak the truth, in love, to someone who does not believe our truth. It will not be viewed as love. Connecting a painful result or situation back to a specific sin is dangerous. Sin, in general, separates. If someone keeps trying to pull you back to a specific sin argument, do not get baited. All sin, from cussing to murder to overeating to adultery, separates. Your sin and Hitler's sin both nailed Jesus to the cross. Do you realize that if even one sin existed in your life, He still would have chosen to go to the cross for your redemption? That is why they are equal, not because we see them as equal, but because He sees them as separating.

I am weary of people positioning themselves as more holy than others. We all do it, but that is not the gospel. The only human better than you was Jesus, and He positioned Himself as lowly. Stop making the faith look bad so you can look better. All sin separates, making us all equally lost and in need of Jesus. Pray today that God will bring someone into your life who needs to hear it.

DAY 31

"There is no arbiter between us, who
might lay his hand on us both."

—Job 9:33

MY HUSBAND ENJOYS COURT DRAMAS ON TELEVISION. HE WATCHES; I sew. I listen between stitches and trying to predict the outcome of the show. It frustrates me to no end when there is not sufficient information, where there is no hope of a guess. I have learned to write fiction. You are to give the reader a sliver of info tying it all together. For example, one of the main characters of my book, *A Day on the Water,* is introduced in chapter 1 without being introduced. Do you know which one?

In Job 9 and 10, Job responds to Bildad. A theme in the entire book is Job being *on* trial while he is *in* a trial. In the first two chapters, Satan pleads his case to God about Job, much like a prosecutor, looking for a way to position his case. Satan treats God as the judge. Notice how in these chapters Job is looking for a judge or mediator to sit between himself and God: an arbiter, a mediator, and one translation even uses the term umpire. Job He assumes God is both prosecutor and judge. But God is judge only; Satan is the prosecutor, and there is no defense attorney. There will always be a prosecutor.

Satan's desire is to direct people away from the path. If you are saved, and best friends with Jesus, Satan's focus shifts from keeping you from salvation to finding ways to make you ineffective in your role. What is your role? Your role is to make God known, worship

Him, and tell others about salvation through Jesus. Satan can never conquer a Christian, even if he or she dies from the trial. If you have God's salvation, you have already won. You have victory.

I feel for Job. There was no Jesus, so there was no surety, no confidence in the outcome. He felt the need to plead his case and justify his righteousness. I am so glad that I do not have to do that, because I would fail miserably. I would come up short, and God would be forced to judge. Yesterday, we discussed that the wages of sin is death or separation. We did not see the end of that verse, which says that "the gift of God is eternal life." We have hope, but not *just* hope. We have assurance of the result: salvation. Do you have assurance?

DAY 32

*"You clothed me with skin and flesh, and wove
me together with bones and tendons."*

—Job 10:11

*"For you created my inward parts; you knit
me together in my mother's womb."*

—Ps 139:13

QUILTERS HAVE A LANGUAGE ALL THEIR OWN. IT IS LIKE WHEN I started working in information technology; there are a million acronyms and abbreviations. In quiltese (the language of quilters), there is the word *stash*. All respectable quilters have a stash. A stash is fabric of varying styles and cuts, stored for future projects or, for many of us, the idea of a future project. It is called a stash because it is often hidden from one's husband. This is because nice quilting fabric is not cheap. Most of us amass a stash because we love fabric. Fabric, while expensive, is an affordable way to purchase art, then partner with that artist to create new art: a quilt. To make fabric, you interlace threads; the nicer the threads and the more threads used, the better the texture and feel of the fabric. Take the cut edge of your fabric and rub your finger on it to see the threads. Are you amazed at how they were woven, each precisely in the right place to make the pattern appear? Think of how much more complex we are than that fabric.

People in the Bible had no scientific means to know about genes or atoms or molecules or any of the scientific things we have today to describe the complexity of creation. Likening our physical creation to weaving was the best way to describe the detail of the process. Do you ever just think about how complex your body is? God took every atom and molecule, after He created every atom and molecule, and meticulously wove them together to make you. The detail of your genetic code, your inward and outward parts, is amazing. Praise God today for your creation. Praise Him for the weaving of every fiber of your body together. Do not be critical of your body today. Instead, every time it comes to mind, praise God for creating you.

DAY 33

"Surely He knows which people are worthless. If
He sees iniquities, will He not take note of it?"

—Job 11:11

REMEMBER WHEN I TOLD YOU THAT AS YOU READ JOB, KEEP IN MIND that just because someone says it, does not mean it is right? These are real humans, living before the Bible, before Jesus, and even before the Church. We need to read some of the friends' statements with as much compassion as we can muster, because while they are wrong, their greatest sins were lack of compassion and their misrepresentation of God. It is easy to make them villains. Be careful—that is what they did to Job.

Yesterday at the store, I met a homeless woman. The temperature outside was below zero! She came into the lobby to warm up and find a charger for her phone. Her dogs were tied outside, barking. Three people came in and said something about the dogs being cold. She answered each time that they were hers. Their looks caused her to grow more frantic. I let her use my phone, but there was no answer from the number she dialed. We went into the store to look for a portable charger and gloves, and to warm her up.

When she left me at customer service to go back to the lobby, a person walked up to the desk to complain about the dogs being cold. I told them that they were the homeless woman's dogs. The person replied, "Well, it's too cold to leave dogs outside all day and night."

With all the composure I could muster, I replied, "Well, she is homeless, and she lives outside. It is too cold to leave humans outside." The woman rolled her eyes and made a snide remark. A society that has lost compassion for humans has lost everything.

The key word in this verse is *worthless*. Zophar believed the mistruth that a human can be seen as worthless to God. This goes against everything that Jesus stood for. Romans 5:8 says that while we were still sinners, Christ died for us. Sin does not make us of less worth—it makes us separate from God. Christ defined our worth by His choice to go to the cross. Imagine Him looking right at you and saying, "You are worth it." How can you judge yourself better than any human on the planet? Christ died as much for you as He did for all humans. This should define all humans as having worth and being worthy of our compassion. Today, take some time to listen to the song "Asleep in the Light" – God bless you, be at peace….and all heaven just weeps.

DAY 34

"Wisdom and strength belong to God,
counsel and understanding are His."

—Job 12:13

IN MY HOUSE, THE BOYS' BEDROOMS ARE DOWNSTAIRS, SO OFTEN WE will holler from the top of the stairs to get them. Generally, when we say "dinner" or something related to food, the response is immediate. When it is chore-related, or a request to stop being loud, or to say it is time to get off the computers, suddenly we are difficult to hear. This causes multiple issues. Interestingly, when they want something, they know to come upstairs and ask. They know not to yell.

There have been three speeches from friends and three speeches from Job since the tragedies. It has been at least eight days since the final incident (seven days of mourning and this is the eighth). It struck me, in my initial reading, that God had been silent to Job. I noticed also that Job had not really gone to God since Job 1:20. He has talked about God, but he has not actually called out to Him. His friends encouraged him to pray, but only to repent of sins that they thought caused God's punishment, yet there were no sins. In Job's speeches, he has acknowledged God's power, authority, and wisdom. One of the tough things about going through a trial is the pain of confusion. Confusion is like a veil over you. You can still see truth, but it is blurred.

In the depths of pain, when hope seems like a distant memory, all your understanding of truth can become blurred. In those moments, cry out to God. I encourage you not to cry out to God only to change your current state, but to give you wisdom. Wisdom relates to strength and understanding. Wisdom reveals truth. It provides comfort. I know that might sound odd, but the comfort of wisdom is knowing—knowing, without a shadow of a doubt, that God loves you, He cares for you, and He has a plan for you. I know that during suffering, those things are sometimes not helpful to hear. The veil of hurt shields your heart in efforts to protect you, but wisdom says, "Release the veil." Call out to God. Pray today for someone you know who is suffering. Send the person a text, even just a simple, "I prayed for you today." It needs no explanation.

DAY 35

"Even if He kills me, I will hope in Him. I
will still defend my ways before him."

—Job 13:15

I FIND MYSELF, EVEN NOW, WANTING TO DEFEND JOB. I WANT THE justification for his words. Maybe it is because I get him. He is, to me, one of the most real and relatable characters in the Bible. He reminds me of Peter: good, but not so perfect that I cannot imagine living up to that standard. Job's humanness is what makes this story work. If Job was stoic at this time, then it would be harder to relate to him.

Even though I love Job, I believe that he is coming at it wrong. Sister, I assure you that I would, and will, defend a Job. I would comfort and console him, and if I heard his friends speaking as they do, in all my Christian love, I would punch them in the throat with my words. Even though I have compassion for their lack of knowledge, there is a time to draw the line. Unfortunately, the same is true for my dear friend Job. While I agree he has done nothing to deserve this, I am frustrated because God is silent. If Job has any sin at all, it is lack of humility and decision to put God on trial. It is okay to question God. It is okay not to understand and to pour your sorrow out to Him. The Bible says over and over that you should "cast your cares upon Him" Psalms 55:22. Sweet sisters, it is not okay to accuse God and put him on trial. As Isaiah 55:8 tells us, "His ways are not our ways, and his thoughts are not our thoughts." I know it is hard.

69

DAY 36

"You (God) would call, and I (Job) would answer you. You would long for the works of Your hands."

—Job 14:15

"If she would call me, then I would talk to her, but I am not going to call her." You know you have heard someone say that in your life. Maybe it was even you. I know I have said it. Stubbornness on my part delays my healing so often. Maybe I took the step towards healing and the other person did not respond, therefore I thought my work was done. Drop the mic, move on, and decide you do not have time for that drama. We can talk about boundaries with human relationships another day, but you see what I mean. When you read the bitterness of those statements, those statements sound immature.

It is hard to read Job 14:15 and not compare it to Jeremiah 33:3. It is the same pattern, the same words, but different speakers. In Job 14:15, Job is speaking, and in Jeremiah 33:3, God is speaking. Context is king. When God says call to me, He promises to reveal incomprehensible things to the caller. In Job 14:15, Job tells God to call him. You could take this verse down many paths. You could relate it to the lost sheep. The shepherd went looking for the sheep, even though the sheep did not ask the shepherd to look for them. God will always come find you, whether you ask or not. God just looks.

This pattern of call and answer is found throughout the Bible. Knock and the door will open; seek and you will find. But the pattern works best when it is us calling, knocking, and seeking. How much are you seeking, calling, and knocking? Today is Ash Wednesday. Fasting or giving up something are good ways to be reminded to seek. When you want something, you pray. You do not pray for the craving to leave, but you pray for the many people and situations in our world that could benefit from your prayers. Lent is a six-week fast. It starts today and ends on the Saturday evening before Easter Sunday. I wonder what God might reveal to you if you gave up something for six weeks, and every time you desired it, you prayed. I wonder what truths He would bring into focus and what healing could occur between you and others. I am giving up some things this year. Pray today that God would help you pick something to give up, so that you can give in to Him more.

DAY 37

"You are all miserable comforters."

—Job 16:2

COMFORT COMES IN MANY FORMS. CHRISTIANS BRING FOOD FOR good times and bad. When someone is born, dies, has surgery, or has another major life event, the food train rolls out of the station. Food is the universal sign of caring, and it is an easy way to provide comfort without saying anything. Once, a neighbor not only brought me food, but cleaned my house and did the laundry. She also fed me scripture. Sometimes food is not an option. Once my mom was in the hospital in a great deal of pain and she asked me to just read her scripture. Once, when I miscarried, a nurse just sat and held my hand quietly. Once, a pastor and my entire small group sat in the ICU waiting room with me as we waited to find out my husband's condition after the heart attack. They coordinated kid pick-ups, they distracted me, and they prayed. We all have stories like these which show that comfort comes in many forms. What are yours?

Sometimes it is hard to know how to handle another's grief or struggle. It is hard to comprehend God's sovereign actions when they do not make sense. Let me give you these three things: being, doing, and speaking, in that order. Being is just being available, whether it is via phone, text, or in person, to listen and pray. Doing is my neighbor bringing food and physically helping. You are the hands and feet of Jesus. Do some laundry; provide transportation for kids.

Finally, there is speaking. For me, it should be last and can be as simple as speaking scripture. Choose wisely and consider Psalms. You do not have to, and probably should not try, to solve their problem or figure out the why. Comfort is like mac and cheese. It is not fancy, but it is warm, familiar, and nourishing. Your words should be the same: a little cheese, butter, and carbs for the soul. Psalms 45:1, 55:22, or 56:3–4 are good places to start. And if words do not come or are not working, go back to being. Sometimes just being there with them is enough. Do not be miserable comforters. Pray today that God will use you to comfort.

DAY 38

"How long until you stop taking? Show some
sense, and then we can talk. Why are we
regarded as cattle as stupid in your sight?"

—Job 18:2–3

I WAS HAVING LUNCH WITH A FRIEND WHO DID NOT SHARE MY BELIEF system. He kindly peppered me with questions about "winger issues." Winger issues are the political ideas that pull strongly right or strongly left. My answers surprised him, mostly because of how winger people present themselves online, or how the world portrays people of faith. After a bit more prodding, I finally told him that I have lived too much life on both sides of that line to judge another who is on a journey that I do not fully understand. I can be strong in my moral convictions, without being judge and jury. The Holy Spirit's job is to convict someone to change. When we put ourselves in His position, we risk being the one in sin.

Look at the second of the speeches by Job's friends. They all call Job a windbag (15:2), which is mistake number one. When you are confronting someone, do not call the person names or say his or her words are worthless. Listen to the person. It should be easy. Why are you not curious about him or her as a person? Get to know the person's story. If you can, take the time to know the person and connect with him or her. Then describe God's love. Care first.

Mistake number two is that Job's friends believe there is no way Job could be right. They believe that they know God so well that there is no way Job is right. Friend, whether you are talking to a believer or a nonbeliever, this mindset is wrong. Notice I did not say God or scripture is wrong. My understanding today is different than it was ten years ago. You need to come humbly into difficult conversations. Being humble does not mean you lack confidence in the Word of God. It means if they stump you, it is okay for you to say so and take time to study and pray. It is okay to learn something from someone you see as lost, or simply not as far on the journey as you. Do not be like Job's friends. Do not tear down when you should be building up. Be curious. Be quiet. Love before you teach, which means you may not teach for a while. God will lead you. Depend on His timing, not yours.

DAY 39

"The fear of the Lord is this: wisdom.
And to turn from evil is understanding."

—Job 28:28

"I DIDN'T KNOW!" MY NUMBER FOUR SON SHRIEKED AS HE STOOD NEXT to some very colorful wall art drawn directly on the wall. Being the mom of four boys, we have had lots of incidents and near misses. There have been many times where innocence was proclaimed for flagrant wrongdoing. Whether trying to load a brother in the dryer or hurling a brother in a wagon at the curb to see the sides pop off, the boys' adventures always pushed the boundaries of their known limits. That is how we are too. Before we are Christians, we have an idea of moral right and wrong. It is defined by societal and cultural norms, which is just a fancy way of saying the majority's belief of right and wrong rules. Most of our norms are rooted in Christian values, although that is shifting as our society shifts. Job 28 is a beautiful piece of poetry worth the read. It is called "A Hymn of Wisdom." The last verse is the summation of the chapter, brilliantly boiled down to fifteen words. Wisdom is quite simple. It is rooted in reverence for the Lord.

Understanding is the knowledge and action of turning from evil, and that ultimately feeds wisdom. When I say the word *evil*, I think of Voldemort or Darth Vader or any of many villains. But in this verse, evil is only plain old sin manifested in many forms. How did you define sin five years ago vs today? Are you more aware of it? Do you have better knowledge of what it is? I do. I did not understand concepts like piety or how being angry at someone is just as evil as punching them. Greed is not just wanting more, it is hoarding or withholding what you have from God's purpose. Understanding evil is not going for the jugular of someone else's sin and sugar coating our own. It is recognizing that all have sinned and fall short, and we all are on a journey to understand and get better. Life is easier in community as long as the community is comfortable with each other's imperfections. Take some time today and think about what you define as evil, then write it down. Highlight the evil that is yours. If there are no highlights, then that is a problem. Pray for self-awareness of your shortcomings.

DAY 40

"When the Almighty was still with me
and my children were around me,"

—Job 29:5

"THIS IS NOT HOW IT IS SUPPOSED TO BE." THOSE ARE DANGEROUS words which I have expressed more times than I care to claim. If you are honest with yourself, then you probably have uttered them or at least thought them during a season of your life. It is easier to work in if/then absolutes in our heads. If we do X, then Y will occur, and to tie a little prosperity gospel into our thinking, if we can align logic with situations, it makes the situations easier.

Take some time today and read Job 29. Think through what your statements would be or have been to God. Job taught, took care of the poor, helped the sick, and fought injustice. What are you doing? I went on mission trips, I helped at a shelter, I served at vacation Bible school, I sang in choir, I prayed every day, I tithed. Now read Job 29:18–20. Job is saying, "I thought if I did all this, then God would do that."

Why do you do the stuff you do? This is a dangerous question. If you dig deep enough, you might not like the answer. God dealt with my pride. He still deals with it, with my "look at me" syndrome. It is hard when you do the work not to want the reward. *Want* may be too nice of a term. Instead I *expect* the reward. A reward could be the praise of people, but also the protection and profit from God.

Write down the things you do for God. Take some time to

pray over that list. Pray that God would reveal to your heart your motivation. It may not be on the surface or apparent to you. Job could not understand why all his ifs had not resulted in positive thens. God chose him to be the lesson for us. Ifs and thens do not line up all the time. Pray today that your ifs—that is your serving God with gladness—will happen regardless of your thens.

DAY 41

*"Did not the One who made me in the
womb also make them? Did not the same
God form us both in the womb?"*

—Job 31:15

SOME PEOPLE READ JOB 31 AND SAY JOB IS BEING HAUGHTY OR demanding. They see his list of ifs as prideful and claim that pride was Job's sin because he believed he was sinless. Some believe that pride was his hidden sin that God was trying to work out. I do not believe that. The point of the book of Job was that suffering can occur without cause, and that our suffering allows God to reveal new truths. Go back to Job 1 and 2, where God identifies Job as having perfect integrity, fearing God, and turning from evil. In his suffering, Job does demand of God and put God on trial. That is where Job messes up. It is where the rawness of pain leads to the need for justification. Faith means trusting in things not seen, and sometimes, questions not answered.

Verse 15 screams of Job's internal goodness, because it reveals the internal belief structure behind the action. That is not easy. The other sins Job mentioned in verse 31 hinge on this belief structure. Job believed that all were equally made by God, and therefore have value. Read verses 13–15 again. Not only is Job he talking about servants, but both male *and* female servants. Those verses advocate for racial, social, and gender equality. You can be commanded to treat others equally, as they are, but to believe in treating others equally is different.

I like to balance the Old and New Testaments. Christ's commands are sometimes things He says to do away with. This is not only echoed but emphasized in Ephesians 6:9b. Here we are told that there is no favoritism in heaven. The New Testament declares that Jesus died for *all* equally; that includes all sin and all people. You are not better than someone else because of your gender, race, or status. You are not better then someone else because your sin is diet sin and theirs is regular. There is no such thing as diet sin. All sin is full calorie. Take some time today and examine your heart. Pray that God will reveal places of racism, or places of sexism, within you. Pray that He will reveal places where you see yourself more than someone else because of social status or wealth. Ask for forgiveness and let healing begin in you.

DAY 42

*"If only I had someone to hear my case! Here is
my signature; let the Almighty answer me."*

—Job 31:35a

I DO NOT COOK. WELL, I COOK, BUT POORLY. MY ONE OUTSTANDING
dish is minestrone soup. The only problem is that I am the only at
my house who likes it. So when I make it, I eat it all week long. I like
it with croutons. One time I forgot to buy some, so in my wisdom
I threw a couple of pieces of bread in the air fryer and thought
they would magically become croutons. They did not. They became
strange, partially dried out bread, and when dunked in the soup
became weird, soggy, dried out bread.

My walk with God has been like that bread, dried out and aching
for some butter or olive oil. Sometimes my soul is not a deer panting
for water, it is a dehydrated deer eating a cactus, hoping for some
form of liquid. In Job 31, Job is giving his final statement, much like
in a courtroom when the attorneys make closing statements. Job has
been berated by his friends, and God has been silent. Job feels that
he has presented a good case to justify that his suffering is uncalled
for and unwarranted. All he wants is the why, just a word from God
that explains what he had done to deserve all this suffering. Sweet
sisters, can I tell you that if you are in that spot where God is silent
and you feel dry, do not quit coming to the Word, praying, and going
to church.

Job's suffering hollowed out a big space in him so that God and

His joy could fill it. Maybe in His silence and in your suffering, He is opening a new chamber of your heart to be ready for Him to fill with more of Him. Maybe He is cleaning out a bit more of you so that the space is ready for more of Him. Imagine moving into a new house and it is still filled with the previous owner's stuff. That is how God feels when you accept Christ. He is willing to move in, but He needs to make space. There are locked doors in your soul with rooms ready to be decorated by God. Today, do not ask God why. Ask yourself, *What do I need to move out to make room for Him?* It is time for spring cleaning in your heart.

DAY 43

*"Then Elihu son of Barachel the Buzite from
the family of Ram became angry."*

—Job 32:2a

SEVERAL YEARS AGO, I WAS HAVING BREAKFAST WITH A WORK colleague one day after we had been not just yelled at but reamed out. As I sulked through my fluffy pancakes and ate away my emotions, I asked my colleague how he can handle it so well and let it roll off his back. He told me a story of when he flew helicopters in the Vietnam War to pick up troops, and said, "When you have been shot at so many times, getting yelled at is nothing. Besides, anger is their problem not yours. Your problem is the actual thing that's broken or done wrong, which is what you need to fix."

Nearly every time I have gotten into a heated situation where I was on the receiving end, I think of that conversation. Unfortunately, for many years, I was the angry one, until I was humbled—but that's another story.

The word used in Job 32 is *hara*, which means to glow or grow warm. A fire starts with a little spark. Think of how you roll a stick and eventually a fire starts from the friction. That little ember only needs a bit of air and fuel to become a flame. That is how anger works. Elihu did not show up to this situation angry, but something inside him was triggered by what he heard. Some may say a passion for God made him feel the need to leap into action. But when someone reacts in anger, it is more about the individual's insecurities than the actual situation.

A counselor once told me to experience the emotion fully when it comes, for just a moment, but do not feed it or fan it with your internal stories of what ifs or perceived whys. Instead ask yourself, *Why am I angry?* Then identify the validity of the what-ifs of your story. Anger is a natural human response to a situation, like the fight or flight response. Eighty percent of the times that you get angry have nothing to do with safety. You need neither to fight nor fly.

When it comes to biblical arguments, anger is not the answer. Humility and compassion go a lot farther than yelling and posting in all caps on Facebook. People justify their anger by saying Jesus flipped tables. Last time I checked, you are not Jesus. Jesus was purifying the temple as part of prophecy. He was angered at the followers of God who were taking advantage of others. Don't use that story to justify your anger or actions. Pray today that God will reveal areas of anger that you should quit feeding.

DAY 44

"It is not only the old who are wise or the
elderly who know how to judge."

—Job 32:9

"It's not the age, it's the mileage." That is one of my husband's favorite sayings. He is usually saying it about himself. We have crammed a lot of life into the last ten years. Experiences can provide us with some elements of understanding, but I would say they give perspective and not wisdom.

Elihu is an interesting character. He is not included with the three friends who traveled, tore their clothes, and sat for seven days in silence. It is important to remember that about the other three. They may have had it wrong, but I believe they loved Job dearly. Elihu was probably stopping by to pay his respects. His name means "He is my God," and based on his response, he is passionate about his name.

Read verses 6–9. They remind me of 1 Timothy 4:12, which says, "Do not let them think little of you because you are young, instead be their ideal." While the sentiment is similar, the positioning is different. In Timothy, young people are instructed to live in a God-honoring way. In Job, Elihu says that just because someone is old does not mean he or she is wise. Wisdom is imparted from God; it is not earned by years. Knowledge and perspective come from years. Elihu describes wisdom beautifully as the spirit in a man. Spirit in Hebrew is *ruah*, which means spirit of the Lord or breath. The word for breath of the Almighty is *nesama*, which is the same word used in Genesis

2:7 when God breathed life into Adam. Elihu says that just because someone is older does not mean he or she has the right perspective. I would add that just because someone is young and fresh and has a nice Instagram, does not mean that person should be listened to either. Wisdom comes from God Himself. We all have access to it if we would just take time to read our Bibles. We need to really read it, not just glance at a verse or rely on others to interpret it for us. Pray today for wisdom, real wisdom, and thank God in advance for what He will provide. He is faithful.

DAY 45

"But I tell you that you are wrong in this matter,
since God is greater than man."

—Job 33:12-13

IN HIGH SCHOOL, I WAS ON A DEBATE TEAM. I HAD A GREAT PARTNER. A competition consists of someone stating a thesis and defending it. It is a timed back and forth, where each statement must be backed up with a reputable article. An individual's opinion means little unless eloquently presented. It was in debate that I learned to listen, read a room, and persuade.

Have you ever taken time to think through how to discuss faith with someone who has a difference in belief? One of the first things you are taught in debate is that you need to be able to win, no matter which side of the thesis you are on. Winning takes more than looking at things objectively, more than passion, and more than putting yourself in someone else's shoes.

Elihu is giving a rebuttal for the three friends. In Job 32:12, he claims that Job won against them. No one proved Job wrong or refuted his arguments. Elihu goes on to claim equality with Job, both having been pinched off from clay as created beings. Then he repeats something Job said, proving that he listened and took note. Finally, he states what I see as his thesis: God is greater than man. It is a meaty statement in this situation. It says God knows more than we do, and our situation is always part of His greater plan.

When you disagree with someone's belief structure, try Elihu's approach. Listen. Do not just pretend to listen. Do not just think about what you are going to say next while the other person is speaking. If you do not actively listen, then you will miss the salient points of his or her thesis. Why does the person believe what he or she believes? Elihu listened so well that he quoted back what Job said—not just summarized, but quoted.

Second, claim equality. Too often Christians claim superiority because of their salvation. Salvation proves just the opposite. We are all equally lost, equally flawed, equally created, and equally designed with purpose. Therefore, we are equally valuable enough to die for, and we are not able to do anything, except to ask for salvation. Salvation is a gift. Pray today that God will bring someone for you to listen to, then listen more than you speak.

DAY 46

"For God speaks time and again,
but a person may not notice it."

—Job 33:14

"WHAT ARE YOU WAITING FOR, A BUBBLE IN YOUR BELLY?" My brother, Gary, would ask me, and I would laugh most of the time. But, sometimes, I would get irritated with him and yell, "Yes, I want some form of physical clear direction on this one!" Then he would always laugh at me and say something about praying more and trying to figure it out less.

Do you ever feel like some people seem to just have an open faucet in receiving God's direction? God seems to speak to them regularly, while you are just waiting for Him to snail mail you some instructions. Job 33:14 talks about God speaking through a dream. I will be honest—God does not teach me that way, unless His message has something to do with a giant hamster chasing me through the streets of New York. (That might have been the spiedini I ate last night.)

He does speak to some people through dreams and visions. More commonly, He speaks through His Word, and through people, prayer, and the Holy Spirit.

The Holy Spirit seems to frighten some people. The Holy Spirit explains the unexplained, knowing when your heart is moved. Jesus said He would leave a Helper and that Helper is the Holy Spirit. For me, hearing the Holy Spirit most often occurs through music; singing is a way I connect. When I lost my voice for over a year, it was torture. I learned how to pray more deeply than ever because I longed for that connection. Prayer is talking to God and listening, and being still.

He speaks through His Word. That means you read, and truth is revealed. Every scripture is God-breathed. Remember that breathing means giving life (2 Timothy 3:16). I study to get revelation. I always want to confirm that I am understanding His Word, not just assuming I know.

Another way God speaks is through people. Make sure the people are not just believers, but praying believers who are in the Word of God. I know that God can use anyone to deliver His message, but my most clear revelation has come through other believers. How about you? How does or has God reached you? What is your favorite scripture in which God revealed Himself to you?

DAY 47

"But no one asks, where is God my Maker,
who provides us with songs at night,"

—Job 35:10

WHEN I AM IN A STORM, NIGHTS ARE ALWAYS THE HARDEST. IT IS harder to phone a friend when it is dark. That makes me always feel more alone. My mind races and replays the day like a movie. I pick apart my inadequacies or tomorrow's projects. It is quiet. I sometimes hate quiet.

Can you imagine Job's nights? The kids are gone, the wife has left, and he literally has nothing. His tomorrow seems hopeless because that is what his today is. I wish Elihu had approached his statement differently. Songs heal, lift, and comfort, unlike any other medium. God designed us to need music. We physically and emotionally respond to it. Worship is one of the most healing things you can do. Sometimes it is hard. We sang "How Great is our God" (on retro Sunday), and I remembered when I was going through my divorce that it was one of the songs that kept coming up. I could not sing it. In fact, I would mouth off to God with something like, "You are not so great—look at the mess I am in." That song just kept coming and kept coming. When I finally broke and sang it, it was like someone washed the acid from my skin and stopped the burning. "Name above all names, worthy of all praise, my heart will sing how great is our God!"

So today, make yourself a little playlist. Listen today to Vertical Church Band's "Psalm 96." Read the psalm with the music in the background. Listen to "Do it Again" by Elevation Music. Listen to "So Will I" and "Champion" by Bethel Music. Rock out to Lauren Wells' "Famous" (the version with do it again ending). Finish with "The Story I Will Tell" by Maverick City Music. Let music be your salve today. Let it bring joy to your morning.

DAY 48

"God rescues the afflicted by their affliction;
He instructs them by their torment."

—Job 35:15

WHEN I WAS LEARNING TO SWIM, MY DAD WOULD STAND IN FRONT OF me. When I got closer, he would step back. As he moved, he would splash his hands in the water, making bubbles and water fly in my face as I neared him. He would call, "Swim to me Bo-bo." (Yes, that is my nickname.) As soon as I would get close, he would do it again and step back. I felt like I was drowning. In today's culture, someone probably would have called the Department of Family Services. That is why when I did it to my kids, it was in the privacy of my own pool. The result was not only can I swim, but I swim well. (I don't like to get my hair wet, but I can swim) My dad put me through a difficult time to make sure that, if I got in a difficult situation, I could get myself out. He applied the same concept in business. He would say, "Well, that was an expensive learning experience."

Elihu got this one right. Even though he thought that Job's suffering was wrong, his statement was correct. God used affliction and torment to rescue and instruct. Regardless of the why, any pain or trial can educate us. Remember that one of the things you can do when studying a concept in the Old Testament is look in the New Testament to see what it says about it. Look at James 1:2–4: "Consider it great joy when you have a trial." It does not say be joyful; it says consider it great joy or consider it valuable. Why? It tests and develops endurance. Why is that important? "So that" (I love that phrase, because something good follows it) "you may be complete, mature and lacking nothing."

If you are in a trial, take some time today and ask, "What can I learn?" If your why is not self-inflicted, that can be hard. I am most often not Job in my suffering. Mostly I endure self-inflicted pain. Figuring out what you are supposed to learn is important. Make a list. For example, my voice loss yielded humbleness, patience (I hate that lesson), quietness, and thankfulness. The list is longer, but you get the picture. Losing my brother—I am still working through that. What things are you learning?

DAY 49

"Listen to this, Job. Stop and consider God's wonders.

—Job 37:14

IF ONLY THE VALLEY WERE NOT SO DARK. THIS WEEK, SEVERAL PEOPLE have reached out about their valleys. These valleys have included illness, loss, wayward children, financial struggles, family unrest, and wounds that just do not seem to heal. As I was praying over these things, I found myself saying, "Lord, if only the valley were not so dark."

Read Psalm 23. It says, "Even though I walk through the darkest valley." I always envisioned the valley as an open space surrounded by mountains. I could not figure out why the valley was bad, except for the idea that it was dark. I might like to vacation in a valley, some place with a great view and a nice breeze. The Hebrew word for valley is *gay*, which means deep gorge. To envision it, look at the letter V. That is a picture of a gorge. The sides are steep, and the base is narrow. In a deep gorge, there is no grass, just rock. It is narrow, so the sun cannot reach it. The wind whips through relentlessly. The walls are rocky and cold. It feels tight and hopeless. Imagine pushing through the narrowest space and the walls crumble, with falling rock striking you. That is the valley. I know it is hard.

Elihu foreshadows chapter 38, which is my favorite because it got me through a lot of valleys, once I understood it. When you are in the valley, it is hard to see the wonders of God. It is hard to see the good and beautiful works of creation, friends, and family. It is hard to remember who God is when you can barely see a light creeping though the end of the gorge. It is hard to remember that He is there. I confess to you that when I was in the valley, sometimes my prayers would start, "If You are even there," and sometimes my thoughts would say, "He isn't there." Mostly, I said, "You have abandoned me." I would venture to say that some of you have been there. It is okay to hurt.

If you are sad, angry, or just numb, take some time today and consider the wonders of God. Take a walk and really look at the sky. Who put the clouds in place? Who tells them where to move? Surrender your hurt to the One who is powerful and heals. I am praying for you.

DAY 50

"Who obscures my counsel with ignorant words?"

—Job 38:2

"GOD SHOWED UP" IS ONE OF MY FAVORITE LINES IN *FORREST GUMP.* Forrest is telling the story of an angry Lieutenant. Dan, who constantly rolls his eyes at the idea of God. As a storm came, Dan screamed at the sky, daring God to sink their boat. Terrified, all Forrest could do was watch the interaction. God did not sink their boat, but He did allow every other boat in the harbor to sink.

Job 38:1 says God Himself showed up in a whirlwind to respond to Job. His first statement was focused on the friends. This may be debated, but think through the whole story. Who is obscuring God? The word *obscure* means to hide or make blind or darken. We sing, "I was blind and now I see." What is interesting is our innate blindness. This is the blindness that is naturally part of the human experience, prior to our knowledge of Christ, and is different than this blindness. This blindness is brought on by someone's ignorance being verbally vomited out. Think about the statements made by Job's friends, not only the content, but the volume of words. Think about the energy or emotion they had behind them. It can only be described as vomit: stinky, nasty, chunky vomit. God calls their words ignorant. *Ignorant* means without knowledge. It does not mean they are inherently dumb. It is not slander. God is not making fun. He is pointing out their lack.

God is asking who just word-vomited things they do not understand

and caused the truth to be hidden from His friend, Job. The intention of Job's friends was good, but they lacked understanding. How many times have I passionately spoken something to someone else, in the name of defending God or proclaiming, only later to figure out that I was wrong? Oh, I hate that. We have the benefit of the Holy Spirit and the Word of God to daily bathe ourselves in truth. Friends, we have little excuse if we are acting like Job's friends. Pray today that the Holy Spirit will lead you whenever you feel the need to speak God's truth to another. Pray for boldness when those moments come and pray for compassion. Pray for humbleness since you may not know everything.

DAY 51

"Then the Lord answered Job from
the whirlwind, He said:"

—Job 38:1

IT HAS BEEN HARD FOR ME NOT TO JUMP AHEAD TO JOB 38. HERE GOD finally speaks to Job. Have you ever had a baby get worked up or injured? The baby gasps for air or holds his or her breath. The baby's face turns inhumane shades of red, and tears will not release from the baby's eyes. The buildup of hurt bubbles to the surface, but it is not released. I used to blow in my baby's face and say, "Breathe." That little puff of wind startled the child enough to allow the release.

Metaphorically, God showed up in a whirlwind, one big breath in his child's face, to release the cycle of stories that Job and his friends were repeating. He showed up so that He could level-set and provide truth. He does not explain why in this chapter. So if you are looking for some level of closure for Job himself, you are not going to get it. Job never finds out why. We, as the readers, can infer why because we have more information. We saw the conversation between God and Satan. But Job himself is left with nothing.

Have you ever felt that way about a situation? Something makes absolutely no sense at all, even years after it occurs. Most often this has to do with someone hurting the innocent, or the death of someone whose removal from the world at that time makes no sense. It could be something like your character being called into question or being tossed into hard times. We all go through bleak seasons of life, and response is important. Job spent several chapters yelling at God, "Answer me!" and "Tell me why!" and "Admit that you were wrong in your action, because I deserve no punishment!" He put God on trial when he demanded a third party to come in and judge God's actions. He stepped out of line, but I have too.

The lesson that God is about to impart on our friend Job comes in the form of one of the most beautiful poems of all time. The lesson is faith. Hebrews says, "Faith is the assurance of things hoped for and the essence of things not seen," or when our five senses say there is no proof of reality. This chapter in Job has fifty-three questions that help you define God's power and wisdom. They help you trust an unseen God through things that we encounter.

DAY 52

"While the morning stars sang together and
all the sons of God shouted for joy?"

—Job 38:7

In Job 38, there are sections of four and five verses. As you read it and it shifts from one topic to another, stop, take a breath and think about what the topic is. Think about why God put it there in that sequence, and what does it make you think and feel. I know sometimes asking myself how something makes me feel seems hokey. I will be honest—a few times I have asked my best friend, "How should I feel right now?" Some of you may say, "Oh, I get the feels all the time and don't need to ask." Can you define your feeling? Start with the general: I feel sad, happy, angry, or content. Now take some time and write down at least three levels for each. Using a thesaurus is more fun with fun words. Then when you read something, look at your list and ask, "How do I feel?" If the "feel" you are in is not on the list, add a new one.

For example, this section in Job 38 is about how God architected the world, and how the angels and stars sang in joy at His work. The topic is God creating, not just painting, but planning, measuring, and designing the world. It is God facilitating complexity and being cheered on by the heavenly hosts. Why did He put this section in this part of the Bible? It is the foundation and beginning to establish that He is the all-powerful creator. It makes me feel awe-inspired and safe. If He did that then, what can't He do to save me? If He architected the whole thing, then He knows and architects my life too! Being awe-inspired is intense joy for me, joy in the idea that I worship and serve the Creator and Founder of this world. I am overwhelmed with joy that He who measured the dimensions of time and space cares enough to hear me, to love me, and desires to be connected to me. Pray today a prayer of worship and praise to the God who planned it all so carefully that every single piece works together for His purpose! Hallelujah! Praise! Hosanna!

DAY 53

"Who enclosed the sea...when I declared:
"You may only come this far, but no
farther; your proud waves stop here."

—Job 38:8a and 11

IN JOB 38, GOD USES WATER TO DESCRIBE HIS POWER IN THREE sections. Read verses 8–11, 16–18, and 22–30. The first two are oceanic references, and the last one (which could be broken into two) is a freshwater reference. Why is water imagery so important? Water is something that all five senses can experience. The verse that strikes me is the one asking who tells the waves "you may only come this far, but no farther?" Think of that applied to your life. The simple analogy is that your life is a journey and at some point, God determines when the journey stops. I think there is more here. Close your eyes and imagine the vastness of the sea, the waves rolling on the shore, and being sucked back out to the depths. Science tells us that waves are a manifestation of oceanic energy. That energy is mainly caused by wind blowing across the surface of the water, urging it forward and balancing the earth's gravitational pull. It is a constant push and pull.

We are the wave. The Holy Spirit is constantly pushing us forward and our human self is constantly pulling us back. In my mind, I see God blowing on the water, His energy entering it and creating a force. His breath gives life and direction. His breath is the Holy Spirit, urging us to do the things we are called to do. We are not to sit by and watch a lost and fallen world move farther from the One who loves the people in it beyond measure. We are on mission with God to reveal Him to the world. Our flesh, responding in fear and selfishness, pulls us back.

Have you ever felt the undercurrent of a wave? It is so strong. I remember once grabbing one of the kids and yanking him from the water when he was caught by it, and then nearly losing my footing. The pull of this world is so strong. Galatians 5:17 says that the flesh (our sinful nature) sets its desires against the Spirit and the Spirit against the flesh. The harvest is plentiful. He desires more laborers. He needs you! Pray today that God will use you for His glory.

DAY 54

*"Have you ever commanded the morning or
assigned the dawn its place, so it may seize the edges
of the earth and shake the wicked out of it?"*

—Job 38:12

I WENT TO THE FUNERAL LAST NIGHT OF A WOMAN WHO SERVED IN the children's department of the church I grew up in for more than thirty years, not as an employee but as a volunteer. A story was told about how she would stay up sometimes until two o'clock in the morning cutting things out for the littles. The song "Thank You" was played at the funeral. One by one, individuals came from as far as the eye could see. Each life somehow had been touched by her generosity. People began to stand. It was beautiful. She was a true laborer. Can you imagine how many kids she impacted over her thirty years of service? That is not to mention the youth and adults she impacted. I know that even if there was not a great reward in heaven for this work, she still would have done it. That is the faith I want.

While this scripture is talking about the literal dawn and it is God explaining to Job who He is, this word picture is amazing to me. I love the part "so it may seize the edges of the earth."

Now think about the sunrise, and how the sun peeks up from the horizon. The light trickles across the ground and everything it touches is changed. Not only because in the light we can see it, but the sun (Son) gives life! It causes the spring after the earth has been dead in winter. Jesus is that light for the world.

We are each given a light when we ask Jesus to be our personal Savior. We are asked to be like Jesus. We get to determine how we let it shine. Some of us are candles. We flicker and seasonally illuminate a small circle around us and warm those who come close. Some of us are flashlights. We are seeking for the lost everywhere. Some of us are lanterns leading larger groups and casting light in communities. Think through different types of lights and how they light up a space. What type are you and why?

I want to be a campfire. (Remember how I don't like camping?) A campfire burns and can spread. You can light a candle from it, a torch, or even another campfire. In darkness, it is warmth and safety. In dusk, it is a space for connection. During the day, it is useful for cooking. Pray that God will show you how you are to light the world.

DAY 55

*"Can you fasten the chains (bind) of Pleiades or loosen
the belt of Orion? Can you bring the constellations
in their season and lead the Bear and her Cubs?"*

—Job 38:31-32

I TOOK AN ONLINE ASTRONOMY CLASS IN COLLEGE. TWENTY YEARS ago, that was a new-fangled idea. There was no Zoom, just digital bulletin boards and email. Many of the assignments were to go outside and stare at the sky. The thing I enjoyed about the class was that astronomy is a nice blend of history and science. The professor explained how people through the ages thought about and understood stars. Our understanding expanded as we gained new tools.

God dropped a little science lesson in the middle of Job. Pleiades is a cluster of stars known as the Seven Sisters. They are literally bound together by one another's gravitational pull. Orion's Belt, my personal favorite, is not gravitationally bound; those stars are simply lined up. The bear and her cubs are their own solar system. The bear is a sun and the cubs are little stars, following her around.

Our knowledge of the stars has changed, but the stars are timeless. Our understanding affects how we see them, describe them, and understand them. Stars are very analogous to scripture. Stars light a dark time. Stars give direction when the sun is not visible. Stars are sources of energy. The Bible is the same. And just like stars, the Word of God does not change; our personal understanding and application does. The more time we spend in it and study it, our understanding deepens, just like with the stars. Job looked at the same stars we see, and he was awe-inspired. He did not know about gravitational pull or any of the detail we get from telescopes.

Go out tonight and look at the stars. Thank God for his creation, and the detail of the sky.

DAY 56

"Who put wisdom in the heart or gave
the mind understanding?"

—Job 38:36

WHEN I RAN A COMPANY, MY ABILITY TO HIRE WAS GENERALLY PRETTY bad. The good hires I made were actually referrals. I always see people's potential before I see their risk. That sounds noble; however, it is extremely risky. I have lots of stories. This boils over into all areas of my life.

The word *understanding* in this passage is *biyna* in Hebrew, which also means discernment. 1 Corinthians 12:10 talks about the spiritual gift of discernment, which is the ability to distinguish between spirits. I have always seen this as being able to read someone's true intention or heart. Some people can smell the Spirit on someone else. It is a supernatural knowing. I have had moments, but it is not something I regularly receive. To be clear, this is not permission to be pious or separate ourselves. We are called to reach the lost. They just should not be your besties.

The kind of discernment, that we all can access, is learned. It's like what is stated in Psalms 119:66: "Teach me good judgement and discernment." Discernment can be developed by consistently going to the Word. As you fill yourself with Jesus daily, things that do not align with Him become clearer and you are able to see the counterfeits. The Secret Service studies the real dollar to be able to quickly identify the fakes. Discernment is valuable for all decisions.

My dad once told me that you can do a lot of things halfway or a few things with excellence.

In projects of all sorts, it is important to develop a governance structure. We identify what is important and how we will evaluate. Then if something is presented that does not align, we do not do it. This lets us choose between good and better, and even better and best. Discernment is figuring out God's best for you, whether it is who you are spending time with or what you are doing with your time. Pray today that God will give you discernment and wisdom.

111

DAY 57

"Does the eagle soar at your command
and make its nest on high?"

—Job 39:27

IN CHAPTER 38, GOD POINTS OUT HOW HE MADE AND COMMANDS THE elements of earth, water, and fire (the sun). In chapter 39, He speaks of the animals of the earth. He discusses ten in total starting in Job 38:39. Take some time and read Job 38:39 – Job 39:30. It is poetry. You might play the theme from *The Lion King* as you read, or sing "Circle of Life."

God is explaining that He created every living thing, but He also created a suitable environment for them. What does that mean for me? I am not much of an animal lover. If you ever met my dog, Taco, you would know why.

Not only did God create you, but He placed you where you are meant to be. He provides what you need when you need it. He brings people into your life through planned interactions. He knows who you need and when you need them.

Remember what I said earlier about balancing the Old and New Testaments. How does God talk about earth and animals in each of them? Matthew 6:26-34 describes how God cares for the birds of the air. He provides for them, even without them storing up food for the winter. If God is big enough to make sure every single living thing was perfectly made and put into an environment where it would thrive, then how much more would He do for the ones that He made in His image? That is you! If that does not make you just get goose bumps, or bring a tear to your eye, then read it again straight from the Bible.

Sisters, God, the Creator of everything, masterfully made this world to work for both the elements and the animals. He architected it perfectly. There is no way any of it could ever be an accident, no matter what anyone says. The creatures in each geographical area are just where they should be to perpetuate the circle of life. The weather is how it's supposed to be, so that it supports the circle of life. How much more would God do for you, who He calls His child? How much more of a plan or of providing? Do not just read your Bible and say that was nice. Let it penetrate your soul and overwhelm you. Yes, there is beauty in this poetry, but the meaning is the gift! Pray thanksgiving today.

DAY 58

"I am so insignificant. How can I answer you?
I place my hand over my mouth,"

—Job 40:4

I USED TO ALWAYS WEAR A CARDIGAN, SHELL, AND BLACK PANTS TO work. It reduced the decisions I had to make in the morning. Those kinds of decisions are insignificant to me. I am only concerned that I look put together. Job uses the word "insignificant" when he answers God. At first, I read this as a statement of reverence. He had just heard about who God is in verses 38 and 39. But read verse 2 and verse 8. God is challenging Job's earlier statements. Job criticized God, then demanded an answer from God. Job did not have an answer for God. He knew that he was wrong, but he did not know what to say.

So, then I thought the word implied self-pity. We hear that at church. People are self-deprecating and believe they are being humble. These are not the same thing. Humility is not thinking less of oneself, it is thinking of yourself less. It is recognizing who you are, as compared to God. Self-deprecation is bad-mouthing yourself. Speaking poorly of yourself is not what God wants. He made you and died for you. He believes you are of significant value. If not, then the Bible is pointless. God is not trying to beat you up when you read the Bible. Just because you are not perfect does not define your value to God. All have sinned and fall short of God's glory. We all have one thing in common: we are sinners. Being a sinner does not make you bad, it makes you normal. Do not use it as a badge of honor, nor as a badge of shame. Just recognize that sin separates you from God. Even one solitary sin of this world separates God from man. God is perfect and pure and righteous, but that is not the end of the story. God does not want you separated from Him.

Despite all the fussing and even Job's questioning of God's worthiness and intention, God still showed up. Would you if someone spoke badly about you? I think that sometimes about Jesus. He gets bad-mouthed a lot and yet He still chose, and would still choose, to come and die for you and me. While we were still choosing our way and ignoring His way, He still chose to die for us. While we cursed Him, He still bore our sins on His shoulders and died.

DAY 59

"Can you pull in Leviathan with a hook
or tie his tongue down with a rope?"

—Job 41:1

DID YOU EVER PLAY PRETEND AS A KID? MY MOM WOULD PLAY A GAME with me on long drives. She would point at a building and ask me to tell her the story. Then I would make up some tale to entertain her on the drive. Those were some of my best memories. Later in life, a counselor taught me to use that skill to expel trauma. I would write the trauma out, like a story, and it made it easier to tell her. Then she would let me choose to keep it or throw it away.

Leviathan and Behemoth are two of my favorite characters in Job. In my world, Leviathan is a snarling dragon that can fly in the air and in the sea. He is green with iridescent scales and evil yellow eyes. Behemoth is a giant dinosaur creature with terrible teeth and dark gray skin. The reality is that Leviathan was probably a shark and a Behemoth was probably a hippopotamus, but what fun is that? The passage says that God is bigger than the largest, most dangerous things on earth. To me God is saying, "I am bigger than even the worst your imagination can dream." To me, that is bigger than any real-life dragon; how about you?

One of the reasons my counselor had me write things down is so a story would build in my mind. The actual event can become exponentially worse because we feed it with additional ideas that, to us, become real. We continue the cycle of being traumatized because

116

we recreate the event. Or worse, we bury it, and some trigger will bring it to mind.

Everyone has been through trauma of one kind or another in 2020. Most women will experience, or have experienced, the trauma of sexual abuse, or of being objectified. You all know the list. Our ability to recover is tied directly to our ability to unwind that experience from our mind and not throw it away. We need to lay it at God's feet. Sovereignty takes on a whole new meaning when you apply it to a trauma you have experienced so personally, not one that you created. The counselor had me write stories so that I could process. I wish at that time that I had learned to give it to God. It would have saved me years of suffering in silence. Pray today that God will help you release your hurt to Him. I am praying for you to accept His peace.

DAY 60

"I had heard rumors about You, but now my
eyes have seen You. Therefore, I take back
my words and repent in dust and ashes."

—Job 42:6

HAVE YOU EVER GOTTEN CAUGHT UP IN A RUMOR, EITHER A RUMOR about you or one you have participated in? I used to be known for being in the know in my industry. Partially, people told me things, and partially, I figured things out by piecing together conversations from multiple people.

People forget that Job and his friends did not have a Bible. Their knowledge of God came from oral history. Job was before Moses; before the Big 10 (as in commandments, not basketball). Everything Job knew of God was rumor.

The problem with oral histories or rumors is that they are not always true. We can piece things together incorrectly. We do that all the time at church. We take a bit of a sermon, sprinkle on some Sunday school lesson, and have a little praise and worship for dessert. We gorge ourselves one day a week, then get spoon fed the Word from a podcast or Bible study. Sweet sisters, you must open your Bibles. I hope you are reading the whole chapter as we go, or it becomes rumor. What is the problem with rumor? Sometimes it is true, and sometimes it is false. When it is about some strange happening in the world, true or false, it is inconsequential. When it is true or false about the Word of God, that is a big deal. Some will start rumors with the intention to deceive, and some will unintentionally deceive. For example, someone somewhere said, "God will never give you more than you can handle." People think that is scripture. It is the opposite of scripture. God always gives us more than we can handle so that we can learn to depend on Him and draw nearer to Him. Read the Old Testament. Do not let spiritual truths come to you as rumor. Go to the source: the Word of God.

DAY 61

"I had heard rumors about you, but now my
eyes have seen You. Therefore, I take back
my words and repent in dust and ashes."

—Job 42:5–6

I LIVE IN THE MIDWEST, AND WHEN SPRING ARRIVES, SO DO tornadoes. The sky spins and then drops to the ground, with intense powerful force. We hide—well most of us—in our basements to escape the danger. When it is over, we emerge to see the carnage relieved we when we can do it without assistance.

Yesterday as the sirens blared, I was in a hallway at the school with the baseball and soccer teams, praying silently that the tornado would not choose that spot to drop.

I cannot imagine talking to a tornado like Job did. To think of the physical power of that wind pushing and pulling is overwhelming. I do know what it is like to feel God's presence. Let me be clear: God is not a feeling. He is not an emotion. There have been many times I have felt nothing at all. This is not because He was not there, but because I was not ready or because He wanted to show up in a different way. He spoke to Moses in a burning bush that wasn't consumed. He spoke to others in prayers. He shows up in experiences, like parting the Red Sea, the great flood, dropping the walls at Jericho, rising again after three days, and other fantastic ways. We do not see God directly. We see the effects of God, and we know that He is there. He can show up for you in a sermon, song, or prayer time.

Job's experience caused action. He did not just see God, get the endorphin rush, and say that was cool. His experience caused action. It caused Job to recognize his wrongdoing, turn away from it, and say he wouldn't do it again. Experiencing God should—no, it must—drive you to action: maybe repentance, maybe helping someone, or maybe sharing the gospel. What has been your tornado from God? What did it cause you to do? What didn't you do? Do not waste an encounter with God. It is urging you forward. Do not stop because others did not have the same experience.

Pray today that God will reveal how He wants you to use your experience for His glory.

DAY 62

*"He said to Eliphaz the Temanite: "I am angry
with you and your two friends, for you have not
spoken truth about Me, as My servant Job has,"*

—Job 42:7

I LOVE A MEATY PASSAGE LIKE JOB 42:7–9! IT IS LIKE SITTING DOWN
to a big dinner with all the fixings! This verse is the salad and roll
that you get first. Eliphaz and his buddies did the mic drop earlier
and said, "We are not going to keep arguing with you, Job. You are
wrong, and we are righteous." God indicates his anger in this verse,
by saying directly, "I am angry with you" I will admit, I accept that I
am going to be wrong in God's eyes a lot. I sin regularly. Sometimes
I even decide to sin—I like French fries and speeding. In my mind, I
see God rubbing the sides of His head and thinking, *Girl, you know
better.* He zaps my scale and I repent.

All joking aside, all sin is equal and separating. Sin is what caused
Jesus to go to the cross. The sin of leading someone astray or making
someone question his or her faith does not just grieve God, it makes
Him angry. Look at Romans 14 and 1 Corinthians 8:13. Paul is
addressing eating foods that others believe are unclean. Under the
new covenant of Christ, bacon is all good. (As an aside, Paul was
actually talking about food that had been sacrificed to idols.) Paul
knew that idols were nothing, so eating food sacrificed to them meant
nothing. It was just food. However, a less mature believer may see that
and be confused. There is no reason to cause confusion over bacon.

Paul was referencing Matthew 18:6, in which Jesus gave a stern warning: if we cause a "little one"—that could be a new believer or one of God's children—to stumble or question or fall away, it would be better to have a big rock tied to our necks and to be thrown into the deepest part of the sea than to endure God's anger. Thus, writing Bible studies is a little intimidating. No pressure.

Job's friends described God with if/then statements and let situation define Him. They said that His love and favor could be earned and lost. Sweet sister, you do not need to earn God's love. You just accept it. He made you. He loves you. Stop making God's love a math equation for yourself, and especially for others. Pray today that God will reveal where you need to examine your heart.

DAY 63

"Then my servant Job will pray for you.
I will surely accept his prayer and not deal
with you as your folly deserves."

—Job 42:8b

JOB IS A STORY ABOUT FRIENDSHIP. HIS FRIENDS DROPPED EVERYTHING when they heard the bad news. They sat with Job as he struggled. They tried to help. They were passionate about saving their friend. Even though they were wrong in what they said, they did try. As that passionate friend in my friend groups, I get them. They walked away at the end. Some might hold this against them, but I don't. They spent from chapter 4 through chapter 28 arguing. Sometimes it is good to walk away.

What does God say about friends? Proverbs 17:17 says "a friend loves at all times" and "a brother is close in adversity." Ecclesiastes 4:10 says that two are better than one, because when one falls, the other helps him or her up. I believe the three friends lived these verses out, or at least attempted it. They showed up! When you are going through a trial, not every friend can weather it with you. Give some grace to friends. Some people are afraid of the storm because it opens wounds in their own lives. Some people cannot handle you dealing with external issues jumbled with internal questioning of faith. Job's friends, while they sounded angry, were reacting to fear, and speaking in fear. This was fear for their friend and fear for themselves. Job's sin had not caused his circumstances. If he could suffer like this, what would they expect in their lives? That would be scary. They were ill-equipped to understand and handle it with grace.

What should they have done? 1 Thessalonians 5:11 says, "Encourage one another and build each other up." Ephesians 4:29 states, "Let no unclean talk come out of your mouth, but only what is helpful in building up and pointing to grace." I know, the friends did not have the New Testament, let alone the New Covenant of Jesus, but we do. That is hard, because we do not have an excuse. God did not give them a pass, regardless of their knowledge. We need to build up using scripture. This may come in the form of correction. We need to listen. We need to hear others and recognize fear, both theirs and ours. We need to have compassion. Pray today for a friend.

DAY 64

*"Then Eliphaz, Bildad, and Zophar went and did as the
Lord had told them and the Lord accepted Job's prayer."*

—Job 42:9

HOW DO YOU STUDY SCRIPTURE? I READ THE ENTIRE BOOK, MARKING
as I go, writing notes, and asking questions. I listen to or read studies
from lots of different perspectives. Sometimes, I even read the
academic, non-Christian type of books; sometimes the authors ask
good questions.

I ask questions about the verses. For example, this verse says they
"went and did," and I ask, "What did they do?" Easy, jump back a
verse. They were told to go sacrifice, and Job prayed. They were told;
then they went and did immediately. What does that tell you? When
God instructs you clearly, do not hesitate. Act, especially when it
leads to repentance. Next it says, "the Lord accepted Job's prayer."
Who was Job praying for? He was praying for his friends, the ones
who were mean to him. He did not hold a grudge and proved to be
a good friend. I wonder if that would describe me? Finally, the verse
says God accepted his prayer. Job prayed off and on through the
book, right? There were times when he fussed (prayed) directly to
God. God did not accept those prayers. He heard them, but He did
not act on them.

Studying the scripture takes time, but it is worth it. Each and
every word, included and excluded, is important. In 2 Timothy 3:16-
17, it says, "All Scripture is inspired by God and is profitable for

teaching, for rebuking, for correcting, for training in righteousness, so that the man of God may be complete, equipped for every good work." It is important to look at the words God chose to put into each scripture. Slow down when you are reading. Soak it in like sunshine. Ask good questions! Ask why isn't something there? For example, why isn't Elihu in trouble? Only three of the friends is in the doghouse. Do you see how one verse can take you days to process if you let it? What is the rush? Let God speak to you.

DAY 65

"After Job had prayed for his friends, the Lord restored his prosperity and doubled his previous possessions."

—Job 42:11

I RESTORE OLD FURNITURE. SOMETIMES JUST A COAT OF PAINT WILL freshen and modernize a piece so it can be returned to its original use. Sometimes I sand and re-stain it. That is a longer, more tedious process, but on the right wood it can be stunning. Sometimes the piece's original purpose is no longer useful, so the change is extensive. I bought an organ from the late 1800s. It had been in someone's barn for many years and had become an apartment building for mice. My dad gutted it. I am starting the process of painting. It is one of the coolest pieces I have ever done. Here is why. Its usefulness had passed—very few people need an organ. Its ability is broken—no more music. The mice did some remodels before I got it. It takes a Maker to figure out how to restore it so it can be used again. Look at a broken, dirty, old organ, and say, "Oh, you will be a useful desk!"

When we go through tragedy or trauma, which we all did in 2020, we can close ourselves off and become bitter that our former lives are gone (like the organ in the barn), or we can figure out how God wants to restore us into something new. God wants to do something new in you. Not your church, not your friend—*you*! The organ does not get to choose what I do with it. It did not choose to have all the things that made it an organ removed so that I could make it a useful desk. Sometimes God removes things from us, even things we love that define who we are, so that He can make room for His vision and plan. I know that is hard and painful. I wish it did not have to hurt so much. He makes all things new. To be made new or restored, you must have lost or been damaged.

I imagine that Job never remained silent about the goodness of God, even though Job never really knew the why. I do not understand everything I went through, but I know I was restored to be useful for His purpose.

So, what is your next step? What is God restoring you to do? How will you make the valley walk useful?

Pray today that God will reveal it to you. Move forward.